The Power of Whole Human
Leadership

Managing Modern Workers
Toward Purpose and Profit

Victoria Pelletier

Published by Unstoppable You LLC

www.victoria-pelletier.com

Print edition ISBN: 979-8-9896797-3-7
E-Book edition ISBN: 979-8-9896797-4-4
Audiobook edition ISBN: 979-8-9896797-5-1

Printed in the United States of America on acid-free paper.

Library of Congress Cataloging-in-Publication Data on file.

Book Design and Artwork by Johnny Lemoine

Victoria-Pelletier.com

Contents

Carpe

Tragoedia

Seize

the

Tragedy

Introduction

Carpe Tragoedia (Seize the Tragedy)

W e are at a pivotal moment in history right now. Between tragedy and transformation, there is an incredible opportunity for leaders to *carpe*, or seize, the hardship and turmoil that has emerged from the catastrophe of COVID—and pushed many of us to our limits—and use it to inspire new ways of facing the future. We are facing a trial that will shape leadership for generations to come.

As a leader, you stand ready to embrace this moment with a fresh and improved approach to influencing and managing the people you work with. In a world still grappling with the repercussions of the pandemic, there has never been a more crucial time to rise to the occasion.

The workforce is ready to follow you *if* you *carpe tragoedia*—seize the tragedy—and make something great from it. I am going to show you how I have done this over the course of my professional career, as well as in my personal life, starting in my youth. This book is not about the pandemic, which I will not mention again beyond this introduction. The behavioural traits and competencies in leadership that I will share with you were part of my DNA long before COVID hit. These attributes helped me stay the course in leading my team, no matter the challenge or adversity I faced.

This book is designed to provide you with the same set of tools and philosophy—which I call **Whole Human Leadership**—that saw me through the most challenging moments of my career. These tools prepare you to emerge from any unavoidable setback, failure, or tragedy stronger than ever before and help you to enjoy a more productive relationship with the workers of today. I extend a warm invitation for you to dive into the profound shifts happening in the modern workforce. It's time to address the demands of today's complex work environment with an evolved leadership style that our world can't thrive without.

What Is Whole Human Leadership?

The Great Resignation and Quiet Quitting were sensational news headlines that caught fire in the media in 2021, describing a workforce movement encapsulating both the huge swath of employees who chose to quit their jobs and those team members who stayed onboard but chose to fulfill only the minimum requirements of their role.[1] Neither movement has helped employees recover lost career advancement, improve job satisfaction, or recoup lost wages. Given my commitment to positive workplace culture and my history of translating adversity into opportunity, I have to openly admit my distaste for the Quiet Quitting movement. In my experience, such a reaction or backlash is not the answer to harnessing a purpose-driven life.

We are, however, long overdue when it comes to cultural change in the workplace. That's what this book is ultimately about—and it starts with you. You are a whole human being who happens to have a powerful seat at the table. As a leader, the modern world is calling on you to answer the resignation and quitting backlashes with everything you've got, as well as to move workplace culture forward in a positive direction. Enter the Whole Human style of leadership. Welcome to the intersection of emotional intelligence and critical thinking. The heart and the head.

The pendulum swinging from relentless achievement to perpetual rest leaves you, as a leader, in hot pursuit of finding that one thing that we have been talking about for decades. It's a term that wore out its welcome years ago because, well, no one seemed to figure out how we could all find it.

Work-life balance.

Exactly.

Ugh. Another term I will admit I don't love.

Rather than recycling this overused and perpetually unattainable term into current times, in this book, I propose a trade-up that comes from making trade-offs and compromises: **work-life integration.** In other words, bringing your whole self to work.

In the following chapters, I will remind you of the biggest gifts you already have and offer guidance on how to offer them up to the world around you. I can tell you that transforming *my* leadership style changed my relationships at work and in every other area of my life for the better. Whole Human Leadership enabled me to reach new heights as a member of the C-suite and as a professional speaker.

"How do you do or have it all?" is a question I am often asked that always leaves me with the feeling that others have perceived my success as a point of arrival.

But my journey is ongoing. The professional satisfaction I get from leadership is now based significantly on the work that I do to advance women in business, members of the LGBTQ+ community, people of colour, and employees who have been underestimated or overlooked. As a leader operating from a place of purpose, I have established a meaningful platform of professional success as an executive for multinational and global corporations, many at the top of the Fortune 500.

It's important to me to support and guide underrepresented people on issues related to, but not excluding, navigating their worth and negotiating compensation in relation to their expertise and the value that they create. As an example, I work with female founders in support of their efforts to raise venture capital. In 2022, female-founded start-ups raised only 1.9% of all VC funds, down from just 2% in 2021.[2]

Over the years, I have mentored many employees and professionals who have sought personal development through partnering with a leader who advocates for them and helps them overcome barriers to their success. Some of the people I have coached have been overlooked due to socioeconomic status or because of circumstantial or demographic differences.

While I know that I exemplify my core values in all areas of my life, there are moments when even the best leaders slip a little. If you stumble, I hope this book will serve as a reminder that you can and will get back up. Whole Human Leadership is a highly personalized experience. That's why I will guide you in creating your own authentic, personalized version of how you show up as a Whole Human Leader. You will then possess the confidence to know that you can use any of your current or past obstacles as fuel right here, right now, to pick yourself up and keep moving forward.

There's a tradition in Japan called *kintsugi*, which is the practice of repairing broken pottery.[3] By filling in the cracks or chips with gold or silver, the artisan makes the piece of pottery even more beautiful than before it broke. As leaders, we, too, have cracks that we don't know how to fill, and we get stuck on how to create opportunities out of adversity.

Much like the graceful art of *kintsugi*, the fractures in leadership in our culture are growing more pronounced, as seen in shifts within the workforce, such as the mass exodus of employees in the post-pandemic era. These shifts may even deepen over time. The real question is, do you wish to transform intentionally, embracing your growth through adversity like mended pottery, emerging stronger and more compelling than before? Or do you prefer to stick to outdated patterns that hinder your progress? I bet that you're reading this book to embark on a journey toward self-improvement, and that's precisely what I aim to help you do.

While "heart-centred," "authentic," and "empathetic" leadership might ring like buzzwords, these are words with great meaning. They carry with them significant responsibility but also grant a level of freedom, deep satisfaction, and personal fortitude you likely have yet to feel as a leader.

Connecting with Today's Workforce

Leadership styles of the past, which encouraged top-down communication, emotionless, boundaryless effort, and inhumane demands, are not sustainable.[4] I will show you how compassion, understanding, emotional intelligence, and self-awareness (to name just a few concepts that I will address in this book) are attributes that are good for business, not just for certain circumstances. We will explore how leading with empathy and authenticity supports stability for yourself and your stakeholders and creates an enduring and natural style of leadership.

Whether you are a new leader, swimming in insecurities behind the scenes like I was in the role of COO at the age of 24, or you are an experienced leader, feeling ineffective and outdated, it's time to take advantage of the massive opportunities you have right now to lead on behalf of your stakeholders. Don't let yourself be held back by fear of your lack of knowledge of *how* to change.

What does that even mean? It means you can stop trying to prove yourself and start *being* your true, authentic self. It means that the friction you might feel stems from past disappointments, criticism, isolation, or frustrations with your team can now melt away. It means that the focus will shift from a singular hyper-fixation on business metrics, like sales, revenue, and profit, to include *people* metrics, which are the real underlying drivers of all those things.

The bad news with the whole Quiet Quitting contagion is that avoiding going above and beyond so the workforce can recover from or prevent burnout may have caused more harm than good.

But the good news is that employees are setting boundaries and advocating for themselves and one another. Are you? They demand reasonable workloads, opportunities to grow, and compensation that is equal and fair. More than ever before, team members want a connection to values, purpose, and impact. Have you considered how reasonable these requests are? When these basic, foundational needs are overlooked and constantly disregarded by leadership, the threat of the silent dissenter looms.

Here's another positive thing: the majority of your team members are not robots, and they sure as hell don't want to be replaced by them. They don't want to quit. They want to feel successful, useful, and valued. Your team has **Unseen Employees** who want a seat at the table. I will introduce you to some of them I have met along the way. As you develop and begin practicing your new Whole Human Leadership style, you will start to see them because your actions impact theirs. When people start to genuinely show up at work, starting with you, talent and excellence rise to the surface.

If you are experiencing high turnover or dissatisfaction on your team, things have to change for the betterment of the entire organization. Temporarily, putting in less effort through quiet quitting might feel like a raised middle finger to Corporate America, but over time, more than likely, most team members won't feel good about it. It's possible that quiet quitting could negatively impact employee well-being, causing a loss of purpose or the self-worth that used to exist in going the extra mile, along with the accolades that followed. And, because we work in teams, quiet quitting can cause interpersonal conflict when more dedicated employees are constantly left holding the bag.

This book isn't about quiet quitting.

It's about courageously advancing.

It's about your journey as a modern leader who is bold enough to be willing to shift from the unconscious methods of the past to becoming a conscious game-changer whom your team readily follows.

No one likes their pasta under or overcooked. Similarly, they don't like their leaders to be too rigid and statuesque, and they don't like them to be too mushy either. Consider this your journey to *al dente*, the middle ground we often lose sight of because we are operating from a place of stress and pressure rather than from self-awareness and compassion.

I don't like to see anyone giving up, but, like any form of

social media contagion, positive or negative, when something catches fire it sends a smoke signal. Right now there's a dramatic need to shift leadership styles. While I think that we should have *always* been operating from heart-centred, human-centred, empathetic, and authentic leadership styles, let's face it, it can feel daunting to be our whole selves at work.

Becoming an Authentic, Dynamic Leader

Enter the anatomy of a leader. In this book, we will explore certain parts of the self that can be effectively put into action through empathic, authentic ways of being. Don't worry! What you just read is not a bunch of mushy jargon being thrown at you. There are times when we need to hold our boundaries and act upon the mission, vision, and values of our organizations. Authenticity and empathy mustn't equate to being too soft. Both are extraordinarily confident, strong, *and* humble attributes.

Underneath whoever is showing up, there are likely reasons you are coming forward in a way that is simply not working. As a young executive, while I wasn't cruel or divisive, I was hardened because I was fearful that I wouldn't be taken seriously If I showed myself as being anything other than a driven, determined woman at work.

Eventually, my hard-nosed approach earned me a nickname that felt completely untrue and out of character for me as a person. (What's the nickname, you ask? I'll tell you all about it in Chapter 1.) I didn't want to be thought of as that sort of person, so I immediately took action to learn how to become a more conscious, wholly human leader and redefined my seat at the table.

This book serves as a rallying cry to understand how the world needs *you* to become the type of evolved leader the workplace sorely needs, and it will teach you how to hone your skills and put them into action to achieve this goal. It's a reminder that we must maintain unwavering commitment and consistency in our practice of personal development until we collectively improve, allowing the flywheel to spin freely and make Whole Human Leadership the new norm.

As leaders, it's essential to grasp and put into action the idea that we possess a versatile toolkit of leadership styles to address a wide array of challenges and opportunities. The present moment offers a significant chance for you to embrace constructive criticism from your employees or feedback from employee surveys and use it as a catalyst for personal growth. If you've received positive feedback, this is also the perfect time to elevate your strengths to the next level. It's about evolving into a complete leader rather than remaining a fragmented relic of outdated approaches. You can even take the lessons from your past, as I have, and transform them into a deeper well of emotional intelligence and empathy.

This is exciting! Business culture is transforming. Gone are the days of stagnation. We are now in a time of movement and regeneration, and you and I get to be a part of it.

While quiet quitting may make for sensational headlines, don't be deceived. Whole Human Leadership is the key to liberating your team from a state of uncertainty and guiding them toward renewed confidence. As a result, your team can excel once more, reaching even greater heights than before, all because you've led them with genuine heart and authenticity.

I think we all recognize that there is no true separation between work and home, given that we are working from bedrooms or home offices so often these days. Sure, we might blur out the background on video calls or use a deceiving stock photo backdrop, but we all know that behind the illusion is an unmade bed or a sink filled with dishes. While we don't have to expose our households to be whole people at work, we do have to admit that we have become poor at hiding. It's time we show up as whole people.

Early in my career, I wanted to feel fulfilled and was determined to make an impact as a leader. I have discovered through my own mistakes, failures, and breakthroughs what everyone is talking about today: that people don't quit companies, they quit leaders.

Through the global corporations and organizations that I have worked for, I gained insight into a vast array of leaders and company cultures, and this dramatically changed the way I showed up in leadership. By experiencing both failures and wins, I grew curious about myself and the business world at large. My investigations were translated into ideas for how to employ both my heart and my head as a leader. Practicing leading through empathy and authenticity was not easy at first, but eventually, it became difficult to be driven by anything other than my core values as a person.

I write this book to help both new and experienced leaders find a different way to build strong engagement from their teams and achieve the business outcomes required by stakeholders. As a long-time and incredibly vocal advocate for diversity, equity, and inclusion, I want to help you decipher that doing the right thing does drive the business outcomes you desire. There's not a trade-off. Doing the right thing is what drives business performance and achievement.

If you haven't acknowledged your past missteps within the confines of current leadership standards, well, now's your moment. That's correct! You have my permission to shout it from the rooftops. Let it out, liberate yourself! As a tribute to the art of successful failure, I'm more than willing to share my own experiences in this book.

This is the perfect moment to extend yourself some grace, recognizing that stepping up requires courage. I invite you to carry your initial motivation for leadership, your purpose, with you as we embark on this journey together.

If you find it challenging to articulate your purpose or if it has faded from view, I encourage you to rediscover it as you delve into this book. Focus on the person you've become today, not who you once were or who you envision yourself to be. You're right here, and you possess the capabilities required. Let's unearth your greatest strengths together.

The world relies on exceptional leadership. To become a great leader, it's crucial to liberate yourself from the shackles of past failure and shame and carry forward only the wisdom gained. There was a time when I resisted vulnerability, so if you find yourself in a similar position, I urge you to reconsider your stance. Becoming a complete individual in the workplace is not only the greatest gift you can offer your stakeholders but also a profound act of self-care, and its benefits extend to all who care about you. It all commences with your unwavering commitment, making no excuses, and giving it your absolute best.

Discovering Whole Human Leadership:
Your Journey Through This Book

Because this is a relatively new professional concept, I am writing this book as a guide to becoming a Whole Human Leader through sharing stories of my own, along with lessons, skills, and traits that define how effectively you bring your whole self to work. Each part of this book introduces you to elements of Whole Human Leadership in the recommended order of practice. Part 1 introduces you to the Incomplete Leader and to the Whole Human Leader to help you identify where you are starting your leadership upgrade journey. In Parts 2 and 3, you will be introduced to behavioural competencies essential to Whole Human Leadership, along with lessons, skills, and mini-practice questionnaires. Also included are key takeaways to assess your progress along the way. Moving on to Parts 4 and 5, you will define your personal Whole Human Leadership style and prepare for the Long Game of Leadership.

I've personally embarked on this journey, and I continue to embrace the Long Game of Leadership in my daily life. I look forward to guiding you down this immensely fulfilling leadership path.

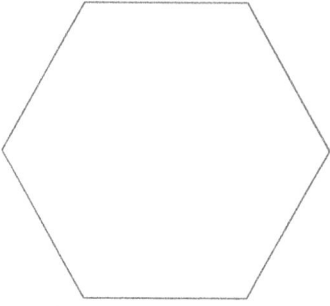

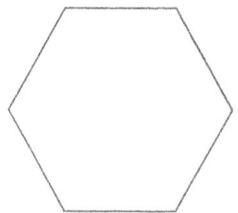

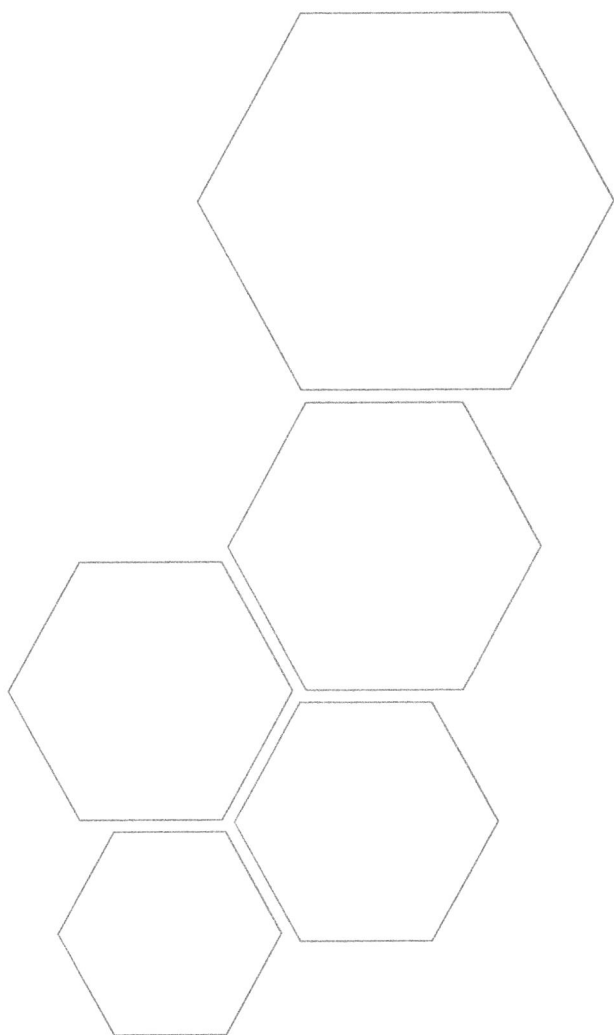

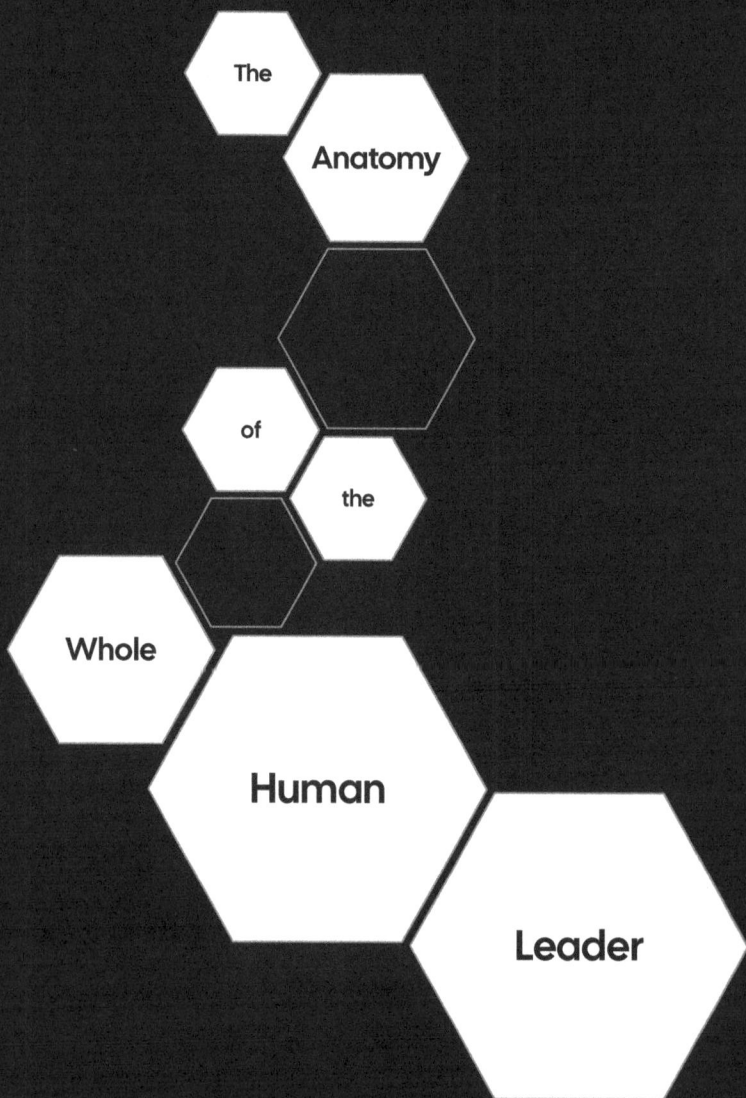

The Anatomy of the Whole Human Leader

"Good leaders build products.
Great leaders build cultures.
Good leaders deliver results.
Great leaders develop people.
Good leaders have vision.
Great leaders have values.
Good leaders are role models at work.
Great leaders are role models in life."

— Adam Grant

Part

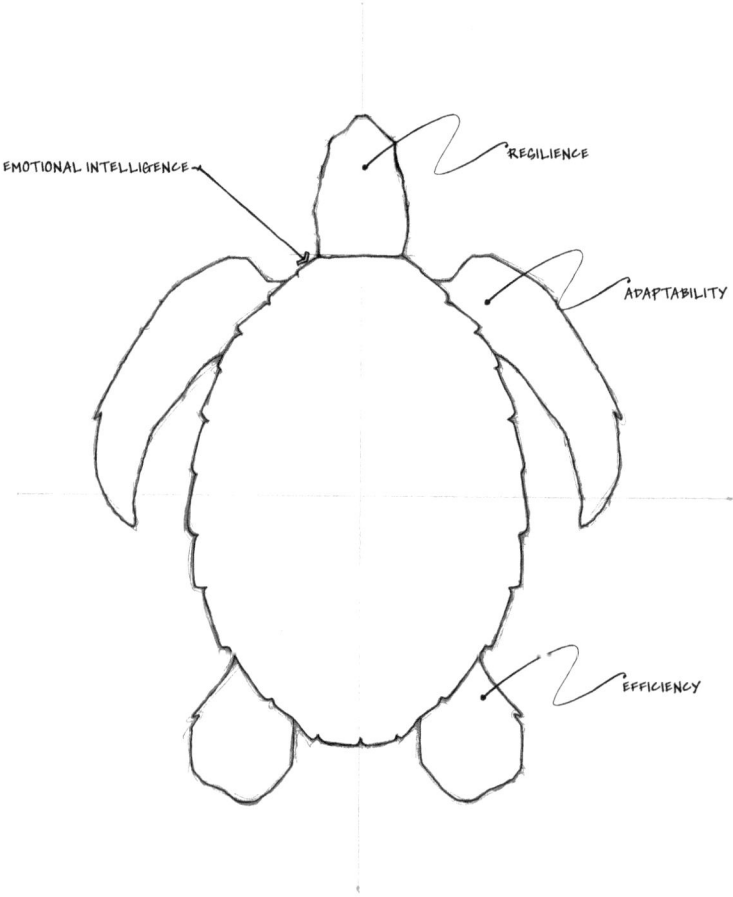

EMOTIONAL INTELLIGENCE

REGILIENCE

ADAPTABILITY

EFFICIENCY

Chapter 1

The Iron Maiden and the Turtle:
Leadership Anatomy

I had heard whispers of the nickname my workmates had given me: the Iron Maiden. While I wasn't thrilled by this moniker, it didn't bother me because I knew I wasn't a *Devil Wears Prada*-type of leader. If you aren't familiar with the film, just picture Meryl Streep in her role as Miranda Priestly, based on a well-known, feared fashion editor famous for saying things like, "Please, bore someone else with your questions." Whether based on truth or fiction, her character's life is revealed over time as a sad, lonely existence.

Like countless others, I encountered challenges on the home front while balancing the roles of wife and mother to two young humans. Simultaneously, I found contentment in my marriage and relished my position as a working mom in the C-suite. My daily routine demanded significant discipline as I expertly juggled various responsibilities, but I was no stranger to problem-solving.

Whenever stress levels escalated in my personal life, I never considered discussing it at work. I viewed my capacity to leave my personal concerns at the office door as one of my foremost strengths. With a determination to excel, I was resolute in not drawing attention to anything about myself beyond my performance at work. I believed that the hardships, trauma, and challenges I'd faced in my life had no relevance to my role as a leader.

Hearing that I was referred to as a medieval torture device (yes, "iron maiden" originally referred to an instrument of torture, not the English heavy metal band!) didn't trigger me at first to ponder if there was perhaps a problem with the way I was leading. I knew that I was leading the business through transformative and, quite often, difficult business actions, yet what I saw was that the team and my colleagues showed respect for me. So, I wasn't alarmed by the moniker. Buttoned up and bulletproof, I continued forward without much thought of being the Iron Maiden until a couple of months later, one fateful Monday morning at the office.

Arriving at work that pivotal morning, I engaged in a polite and typical conversation about weekend activities with a colleague who was also on the leadership team. I told her that I had gone to the movies and that the film was so emotionally moving that I couldn't stop crying. She looked at me incredulously. I noticed the expression on her face. "I didn't have enough Kleenex," I continued. Her response shook me. "Oh, Victoria, I thought you would be the type of person who would laugh at people who cry at movies." That's when the Iron Maiden punctured me with her spikes. Ouch! I didn't know what to say. I awkwardly chuckled and then politely turned and walked away, straight-faced to maintain my composure. I couldn't let her see how incredibly distressed I was by what she said.

Holy shit! Is that what people think of me? Do people really perceive me this way?

Perception is reality, I thought. If this is how people view me at work, I am doing something very, very wrong because I know that is *not* me. I knew that the workplace version of me that people encountered in the office was just a shell of my whole self. But apparently, this was not at all obvious to my colleagues.

My best friend has a nickname for me, too. Turtle. Before I go any further, allow me to clarify that being called Turtle has nothing to do with me being slow. My best friend recognized my resilient nature as being reflective of the physical and emotional strength of the Turtle.

As a child, I endured abuse from my biological mother and was in and out of the child welfare system until the age of 4. From a young age, I discovered that the positive outcomes in my life stemmed from my courage to pursue them. Fortunately, I was adopted by loving parents, but we often faced challenges due to our modest economic circumstances.

My journey to the C-suite at the tender age of 24 was a testament to my unwavering commitment to a "No Excuses" philosophy, shaped by my determination to overcome my past. My loved ones are familiar with my unyielding and resilient side, but they also know that I can be moved to tears by a poignant movie in a dimly lit theatre. They know my shell, and they know my marshmallow-like insides. I love the Turtle label and cherish the dichotomy so much that I decided to commemorate it with a tattoo symbolizing my authenticity on my forearm.

After that conversation with my colleague, I realized that both my childhood and societal expectations and depictions of leadership had made me the Turtle at home while simultaneously shaping me into the Iron Maiden at work. Looking back with compassion on my position, it was reasonable that I protected myself at work. As the youngest executive and often one of, if not the only, woman on the senior leadership team, I decided— and it felt like the world decided— that to reach my goals, I had to wear the iron-clad mask.

There was business to get done. *That* was my focus. A heavy suit of armour, I thought, would lead to more success. And it *was* a primary contributor to my success up until that point. Validation, in the shape of an invitation to join the C-suite and an increase in income, affirmed that I was heading in the right direction. I was deeply committed to delivering exceptional results, and I consistently surpassed my leaders' expectations. However, everything changed during that pivotal Monday morning conversation. It became abundantly clear to me that I could no longer bear the feeling of being an incomplete person at work.

The Anatomy of the Iron Maiden

Upon realizing that I wanted to go beyond my perceived Iron Maiden form and be understood at work as a whole human being, I did a little research. Admittedly, I knew little of the reference. Because I was well-respected as a leader, I considered that the team at work likely drew the same associations with my ill-fitting nickname as I did. I showed little emotion. Truth. I wasn't afraid to make hard decisions. Truth. I did what I needed to do to get results. Truth.

What I found in my research on the iron maiden made me think long and hard about leadership. I began working to make sense of the "Bad Bosses," or the people like me who believed there was simply no way to be a whole human at work. Could a Bad Boss be in actuality a good person cloaked in layers of protective armour? Was I holding myself back at work to the detriment of our team by sticking so rigidly to my good intention of keeping it professional?

The iron maiden is a medieval torture device that was supposedly used to inflict pain and suffering on a prisoner. It is a large metal cabinet with spikes on the inside. The prisoner would be placed inside the cabinet, and the door would be closed slowly, impaling the prisoner on the spikes. The first known mention of the iron maiden was in a sixteenth-century book by the German chronicler Johannes Aventinus. Aventinus described an iron maiden that was used by the Duke of Nuremberg to torture criminals.

When considering the anatomy of this device, I considered that the prisoner might just be a leader like me. Was I trapping myself in a torture chamber of my own making in an attempt to prove myself? As leaders, are we unknowingly undermining our teams and our potential by withholding from them valuable, humanizing aspects of ourselves that emerge only outside of working hours?

Interestingly, there's no historical evidence of an iron maiden's existence in Nuremberg. It's likely a myth crafted to instill fear, serving as a stark symbol of the cruelty and inhumanity of the Middle Ages. Hmmm... that bears a resemblance to the portrayal of the infamous Bad Boss character so often seen in movies and on social media.

Were my colleagues hitting the mark with this nickname? Was I, like the iron maiden, putting up a facade? Did my desire to maintain a strict professional demeanor, aiming to shield both myself and others from the entirety of who I am, inadvertently construct an obstacle at work for my team? I mean, she told me that she thought I was the kind of person who *laughs* at people who cry at the movies!

Let's embark on a journey together to reframe our perspective and replace the term "Bad Boss" with a more constructive and compassionate one. By doing so, we can shift our focus toward viewing ourselves and others as whole humans, acknowledging the full spectrum of who we are beyond the confines of the workday.

The Iron Maiden	The Incomplete Leader
⬡ Spikes	⬡ Criticism, Blame, Distress, Fear, Ill-Being
⬡ Cabinet	⬡ Compartmentalized and / or Toxic Work Environment
⬡ Prisoners (Aware and Unaware)	⬡ Everyone Impacted—Leaders and Team

The Iron Maiden Is the Incomplete Leader

I came to realize that I was focused on being "all business, all the time." I had no time for feelings and emotions, and I didn't invest the time in building trusted relationships from a place of care and compassion. It was my ability to make tough decisions and manage performance, without showing my emotions, that garnered me my nickname. I was doing my job well, based on traditional business and financial metrics. I now know that my capabilities as a leader were limited and incomplete with this approach.

Are you feeling incomplete as a leader? If you are, consider the potential confusion your team may face when engaging with you. Reflect on your own encounters with incompleteness.

Let's break it down and compare the anatomy of the Iron

Maiden to the Incomplete Leader. Note that this relates to both the leader's self-infliction (intended or unintended torture of self) and external infliction (intended or unintended torture of others).

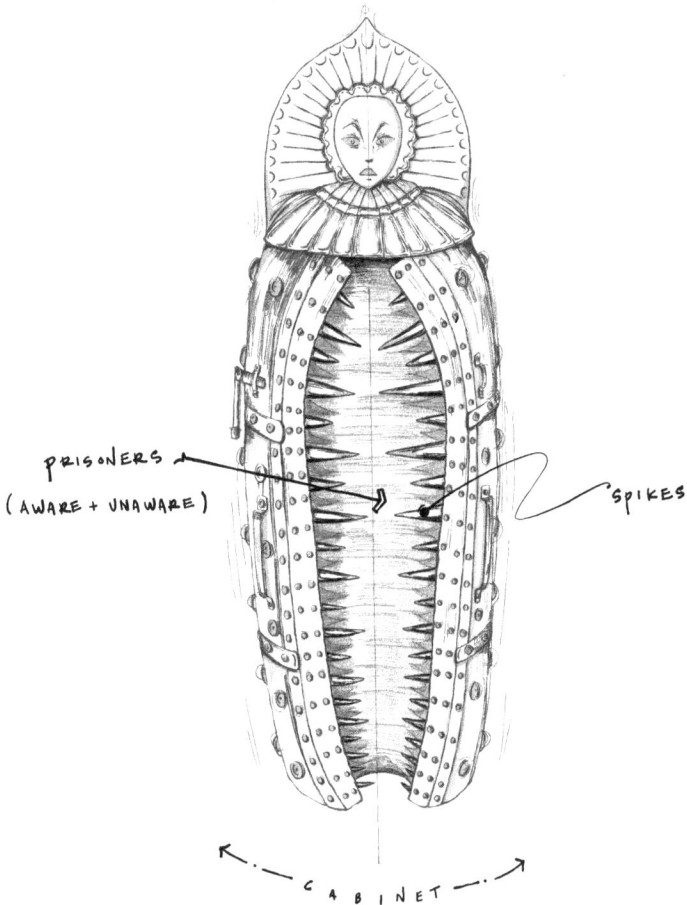

The spikes represent the criticism, blame, distress, fear, and ill-being (poor or declining health and wellness) leaders experience themselves. The spikes also relate to how leaders often, knowingly or unknowingly, project their problems and deficiencies onto their teams.

Incomplete Leaders contribute to the creation of a "cabinet," symbolizing a fragmented or unhealthy work environment. Leaders carry a substantial burden of responsibility. While collaboration is essential, it is crucial for leaders to take ownership of what is built or dismantled. You occupy a multifaceted and privileged position and wield decision-making authority. You also exert significant influence, affecting others to an extent you may not be fully aware of. As leaders, we must acknowledge our responsibility for how we present ourselves. We must be careful to avoid creating a cabinet in our workplace, and if one already exists, it's up to us to figure out how to dismantle it.

My aspiration for you is to gain the self-awareness necessary for the transformation into a Whole Human Leader, enabling you to make informed choices about your daily interactions and decisions.

Compartmentalizing our true selves, pushing trauma and stress into an unseen heavy backpack, doesn't make the weight disappear; it still lingers. Over time, this burden can become overwhelming and manifest in ways that run counter to effective leadership. Incomplete Leaders might find themselves talking over their team members, disrupting employee concentration with an excessive need for work details, or frequently displaying frustration. All of these behaviours hinder the process of adequately guiding and training your team and negatively impact their ability to perform efficiently and effectively.

For me, the journey to becoming a Whole Human Leader has never been about imparting my personal life onto my work. Yet I must admit that the leader I used to be did allow her personal life to affect her in the workplace. How? By allowing my difficult early life experiences to create the tough, invulnerable Iron Maiden persona I presented at work. The good news is that you and I are going to do a lot of unpacking together, so you don't have to live or lead this way any longer.

To reiterate, prisoners of the Iron Maiden are not only representative of your team members trapped in a toxic environment. The leaders are prisoners, too. It's kind of like the common phrase, "We are all in this together."

Isn't it time for a new phrase? Isn't it time we say, "Let's get out of this together."

Just as the iron maiden could cause serious injury and death to its prisoners, the Incomplete Leader, whether they mean to or not, can cause serious emotional and psychological damage to their employees. Employees who work for an Incomplete Leader may experience stress, anxiety, depression, and burnout. They may also feel undervalued, unappreciated, confused, and disrespected.

Cultures that are run by Incomplete Leaders may breed Unseen Employees, what I call the team-member equivalent to the Incomplete Leader (to be examined later in this book).

Exiting the Torture Chamber

My transition away from being an Incomplete Leader did not happen overnight. At first, it felt foreign and unnatural to go from walking into a meeting and getting straight to the business agenda to having a bit of casual conversation and building rapport before digging into the meeting topics. I did a lot of internal self-talk to move myself to take action. "Vic, stop. You need to take five minutes to engage. Ask people about their weekends—and mean it." I realize that my habit of getting right down to it would take time to break up. This meant that I had to practice feeling uncomfortable and awkward.

I always conducted one-on-one touchpoints and performance reviews that encompassed setting goals and objectives. However, I now dedicate additional time to understanding what truly matters to our employees, ensuring they receive not only the support they need to excel and develop but also that they feel seen and valued.

After years of practice, including navigating numerous mergers and acquisitions that prompted frequent moves, I managed to cultivate a remarkable following of individuals who chose to journey alongside me. Much of this success can be attributed to leading through my own life experiences, including the fear of being "the only" at the table or in the room. My journey of transformation was moved along by even the smallest actions I took in those early days. Soon enough, the Turtle re-emerged.

The Anatomy of the Turtle

Knowing that I wanted my work colleagues to ditch their Iron Maiden perception of me and instead experience me as the Turtle (as I was recognized in my personal life), I decided that I needed to look deeper into the makeup of this creature. The turtle's hard shell and soft interior seemed like an obvious correlation to my natural and authentic way of being, but I wanted more context.

Turns out, I was like a baby sea turtle as I transitioned out of my old ways. After they hatch, the baby turtles have to struggle to get from the beach to the ocean. During the process, their lungs strengthen, preparing them for a life under the sea.

Training myself to become the Turtle at work, while difficult, was breathing new life into my experience as a leader.

We read the autobiographies of the world's best CEOs with a similar fascination to that of watching a turtle swim through the sea. Known for their ability to withstand harsh conditions and survive even the most difficult situations, turtles are resilient and patient creatures. Please don't confuse patience with pace. Great leaders are strategic and swift while keeping pace to avoid burnout.

As the Iron Maiden, I held back my emotional side at work, tightly sealed in the chamber. When I got home, I would often release it in moments of intense crying. It was positive that the Turtle appeared at home, but my workplace habit of bottling up the sides of myself that ultimately led to a calm, more connected leadership style didn't do anyone any good.

My experience as the Turtle didn't mean that I would bawl my eyes out in a business meeting; rather, I became comfortable in moments when my eyes did well up or I shared a story about a failure or mistake of my own so the team felt they could safely share their own emotions. Turtle leaders can maintain composure because there isn't a surplus of stored mental and emotional fatigue that's locked up for forty or more hours per week.

Can you recall a Turtle moment, day, or year? More than likely, you can. What's possible, knowing that you can have more such experiences?

Let's break it down together and compare the anatomy of the Turtle to the Whole Human Leader. Note that this relates to the leader's self-awareness (understanding of self) and external awareness (understanding of the world around them).

In addition to the metaphorical comparisons to the turtle's anatomy, Turtles also exhibit behavioural traits that are essential for great leadership.

Through this book, you will go on the journey to becoming your own version of the Turtle. Consider this framework my recommended progression to becoming the Turtle, from the starting line through to the finish.

The Turtle	The Whole Human Leader
Shell	Protection, Resilience
Strong Limbs	Adaptability, Efficiency
Keen Senses	Awareness, Anticipation
Long Lifespan	Commitment, Perseverance, Health
Patience	Problem Solving, Strategizing
Wisdom	Informed Decision-making
Calmness	Composure Under Pressure

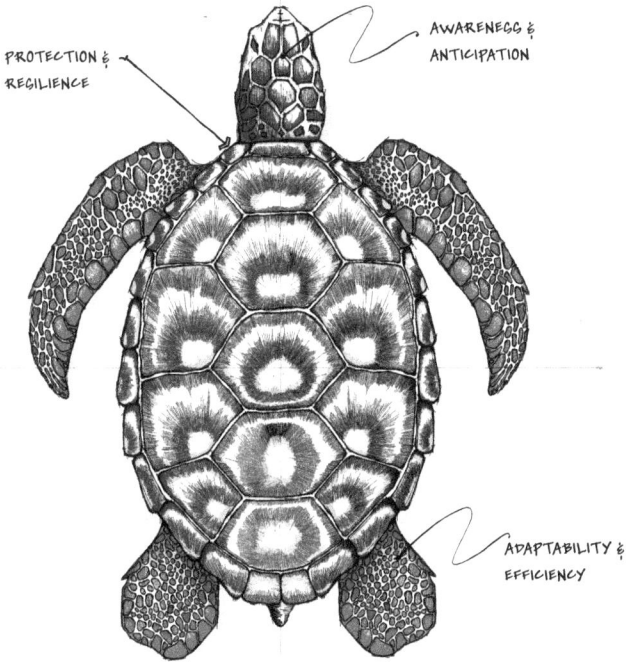

PROTECTION &
RESILIENCE

AWARENESS &
ANTICIPATION

ADAPTABILITY &
EFFICIENCY

The Whole Human Leader	Defining the Anatomy of Whole Human Leadership	The Whole Team
Critical Thinking Empathy	Competencies for Performance	Emotional Intelligence / Authenticity
Navigating Change	Fostering Growth and Resilience	Highly Engaged / Diverse
Humble Successes Successful Failures	Fostering High-Performing Teams	Challenges / Breakthroughs
Personalization	Sustainable Leadership	Evolution

Working on these learned traits and skills will ultimately help you create a high-performing team.

We hide lived experience.

We hide what we think makes us different from others.

We hide fear and insecurity.

We base what we do on the depiction of leaders in movies and, if you are of my generation, the way we have experienced leaders firsthand in our careers.

The Turtle delivers results. You'll come to recognize this as you purposefully and strategically implement the insights from this book. I assure you that if you enhance just one of the traits discussed in this book beyond your current level, you will witness positive outcomes manifest both within your team and in your life.

A turtle, while independently proficient and capable, swims with a crew, or a bale, in official terms. As an Incomplete Leader, you might just be misreading the strengths of your team. Or you might be taking them for granted. Or perhaps you are unconsciously or consciously blind to seeing them. See them and they will follow you. The Turtle steps up to develop high levels of conscious behaviour to set an example for their team.

Chapter 1 Key Takeaways

- *The Iron Maiden shields humanizing parts of themselves in the workplace in an effort to protect themselves. This tends to work to the detriment of both themselves and their team.*

- *Everyone is tortured, including the Iron Maiden, under any type of leadership that is not based on authentic Whole Human interaction.*

- *The Iron Maiden is an Incomplete Leader who is capable of transforming into the Turtle.*

- *The Turtle is the Whole Human Leader who relentlessly uses all parts of themself as a way to achieve self-fulfilment in leadership and create tightly bonded, high-performing teams.*

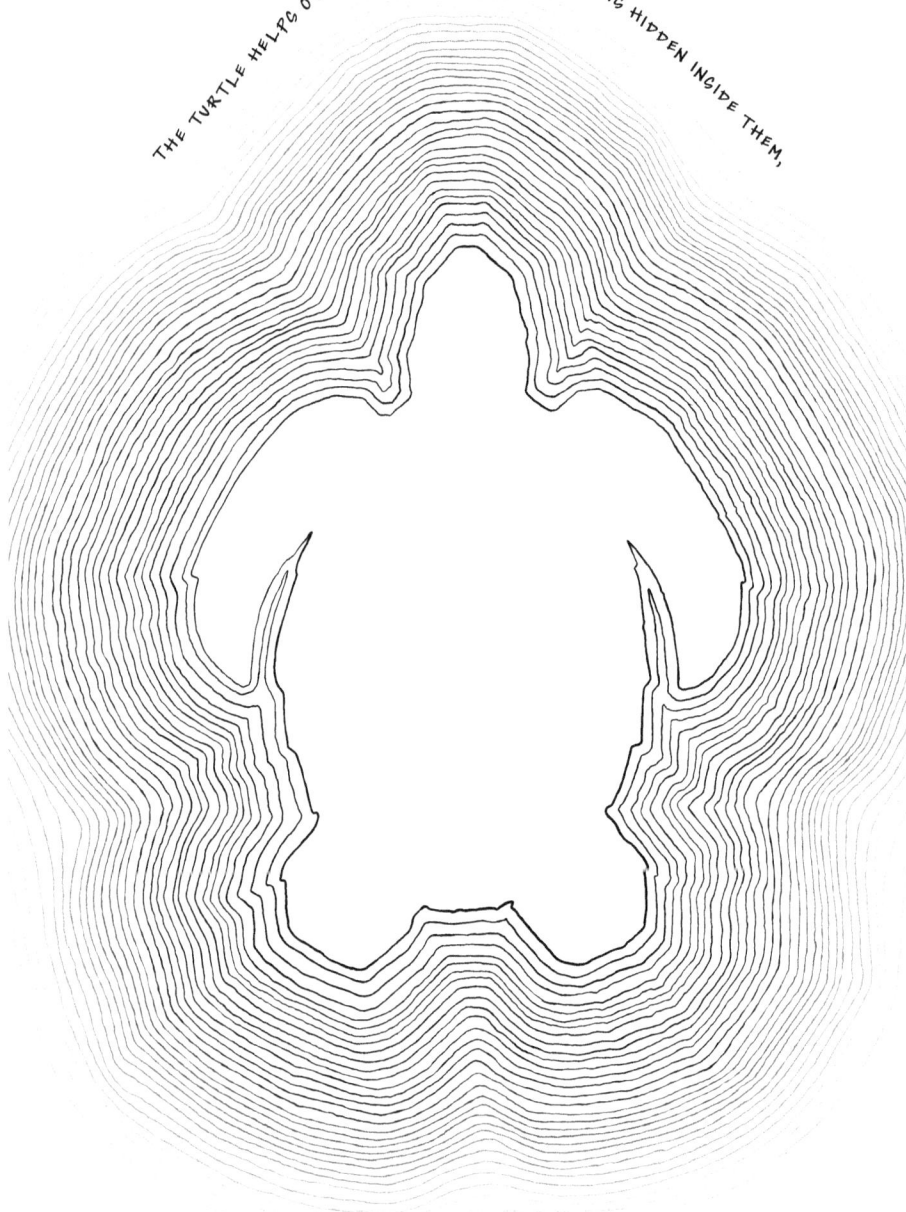

THE TURTLE HELPS OTHERS DISCOVER THAT WHICH IS HIDDEN INSIDE THEM,

THAT WHICH CONTAINS VALUE AND PURPOSE.

Chapter 2

The Unseen Employee: Completing Your Team

T he evening and overnight shifts at the call centre I oversaw as a senior leader before the days I took my first COO position had significant staffing and retention problems. Typically, contact centres, especially those operating in a 24/7 environment, have high turnover. My team, however, performed above the rest, so my boss asked me to help take the stress out of the environment so as to boost the performance of the other teams. Interestingly, during that time, my ex-wife, Dee, worked in the same call centre at night to make extra money, so I had the benefit of additional inside information regarding the state of morale among the staff she worked with. One thing she made clear was that the best part about her work environment was the man who sat next to her.

Dee spoke of David often, telling me about how the usual nightshift doldrums had been turned into a time of enjoyment after he started working there. I met David when I stopped by Dee's desk to chat with her. Even while sitting down, he was tall. Not only was he long in stature, but he was also broad. Having hit my height at a young age, I still feel like I'm way taller than I am, so it's rare for me to ever be intimidated by anyone—but if I were, it might be by David. It wasn't only his height that made him stand out— he was extremely handsome. Gregarious and funny, he broke up the monotony in the call centre. I loved passing through to engage with him. Every time I walked away, I had a surge of energy to make it through my shift.

Many of the staff kept their distance from David, and I heard remarks from some that he was intimidating, either because of his stature or his good looks. There also seemed to be bias at play. David is black. However, once staff members learned that he had been a linebacker in the Canadian Football League, they appeared more comfortable. Dee shared all this with me. Being an observant person, she had a number of insights and direct experiences with her peers and always took mental notes. Many of the things she noticed bothered her, so she confided in me outside of work.

David never said anything to Dee about bias or racism at work. Over time, he became the team Turtle, winning the team over by simply being himself.

Hired as a call centre agent on the front lines, his work day was about one thing: answering the phone. The people on the other side of the phone didn't have the opportunity to see his smile or how he paid attention while speaking to you. But they *heard* it, loud and clear. Clients were not intimidated by David's physical stature, and they didn't know that he was a retired professional football player who had won two Grey Cup rings (the Grey Cup

---

[1.] All names used in leadership examples and scenarios in this book have been changed.

is the Superbowl equivalent in the Canadian Football League). What they did know was that he was charming and warm and that he was great at solving problems. Engaging with people and building rapport and trust with them was effortless for him and a key factor in his team's high level of performance.

Still very much in shape and looking like a linebacker post-retirement, David's body was intact, but his career had to change. To provide for his family, he found a new vocation at the call centre. Compared to their American counterparts, he would later explain to me that Canadian Football League players make significantly less money, so there was no extravagant fund waiting for him after his playing days were over.

David was helping us grow and became a vital player in the contact centre. Early on, I was drawn to put in extra effort to get to know him and understand what he was looking to accomplish so I could keep him engaged.

A couple of years after first meeting David, I was working at a different company and had an opening for a client account manager position. Even though David had significantly less experience and formal skills than other candidates, I hired him for the position.

I knew we could train him about the operational contact centre responsibilities and the client reports he would be accountable for. What I didn't need to train him on was the most important thing of all: how to build rapport and relationships with people and clients. I already knew he had developed the drive, discipline, and social awareness to more than ably accomplish that. Whether he was with an easy-going or difficult client, he simply knew how to effectively solve problems and maximize our partnership opportunities.

Because of all of his years as a football player, coupled with his other personal and professional experiences, David brought so much richness to the team. Without having to fight for it, simply by being himself and leaning into his strengths, he encouraged the more traditional leaders at the company to think differently.

Twenty years later, he's in the same line of work, soon to retire from the second half of his professional career. It was a privilege to have played a small role in giving him that opportunity.

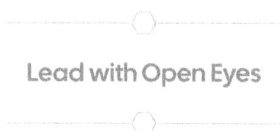

Lead with Open Eyes

My work with David was an example of my growth as a leader, a glimpse of myself as a Whole Human Leader that I would recall years later when I was breaking through the iron cabinet. I think it is safe to say that most leaders have had Turtle moments, and it is stories like this that often come back to remind us that we can operate in this way 100 percent of the time.

To embody the Turtle's ethos, you can't journey solo. Identifying individuals whose skills and enthusiasm dovetail with your strengths and compensate for your weaknesses requires an acute awareness of everyone around you. By staying observant, you're likely to spot employees like David, brimming with passion and focus, yet often overlooking the need to self-promote.

Have you ever been blinded by the light?

Has the top 10 percent of your team left you wishing you could pattern-match or clone them? Or are you hiring those in your own likeness and experience (a practice often called an "affinity bias")?

Much of this can be referred to as hiring based on an algorithm. An article published by *Harvard Business Review* exploring the complexities of algorithms and the connection to bias found that "most hiring algorithms will drift toward bias by default.[5] While their potential to help reduce interpersonal bias shouldn't be discounted, only tools that proactively tackle deeper disparities will offer any hope that predictive technology can help promote equity, rather than erode it."

What do we get when we get more of the same people?

You might think the answer is more revenue or bigger results, and perhaps, sometimes, that's the case. More than likely, alongside the results, you will also get a group-think mentality, a lack of perspectives that stem from similar cultural, gendered, racial, and socio-economic backgrounds and experiences.

For companies to achieve a competitive advantage, diversity, equity, and inclusion (DEI) have to be embraced as more than a moral imperative. DEI, per all the latest research, is good for business. Diverse teams are 45 percent more likely to improve market share.[6] Whole Human Leaders, as I define them, understand that DEI helps foster resilience and growth. We will talk about diversity at length in Chapter 6.

A significant number of Unseen Employees I have worked with over the years have been female and LGBTQ+. Given that my personal experience of being "the only one" was based on being a young, queer female, many of the employees I have coached and mentored over the years have come to me because they realize that I have encountered and overcome similar biases and challenges. My plight, however, is universal, and seeing Unseen Employees across demographics has given me incredible insights into how a leader can and should train, educate, and coach a diverse range of employees to achieve success.

Do you want to be a leader whom an array of people want to follow or a leader whom only a handful will accompany?

Look around your physical and online spaces and diversify your interests when it comes to connecting with the team. The Unseen Employee just might be the key to improving your product or service and improving *you* as a leader and a whole human. When an individual has a purpose that is honoured inside during the work hours of the day, you will be a leader that all people on your team want to follow. Okay, maybe not all, but imagine what that team member whom you have never spoken to feels like once you start regularly engaging with them.

When you walk past your employees, start by looking at them.

There's a fantastic cartoon by William McPhail for *The New Yorker* that I often reference in speaking presentations when talking about diversity, equity, and inclusion.[7] He depicts a woman with long, dark brown hair and dark skin sitting on a chair facing a panel of ten men with the same white skin, dark hair, suits, and ties. The caption reads, "Describe what you can bring to this company."

They are all facing her, but they are not seeing her. None of the men in the cartoon are looking at her. However, in real life, sometimes people are looking, but they still aren't *seeing*. It's these times when you can tell you aren't enough in the eyes of others (important enough, wealthy enough, of appropriate status, etc.). I'm not bringing up this cartoon as a criticism of men. It's a great artistic statement of the Unseen Employee. Consider everyone on your team to be important, to be enough, as you become the Turtle.

Who Is the Unseen Employee?

We can start with the people you may have a tendency to walk by without engaging or those you don't engage directly with on video conference calls. Those already on the team who are right under your nose. You might miss them because you are too busy paying attention to the boisterous, hyper pain in your side revenue producer—the sort who is often referred to as the

"Toxic Top-Performer." I get it. Money talks... but does it? The Unseen Employee likely has talents outside of work that are unknown to you because maybe they have been turned down for a promotion or they don't have a college degree. Unseen Employees can be direct reports. Or they could be job applicants you were never even aware of because their resumes were filed away or red-lined before they made it to your desk. How can you be sure that a "red flagged" gap in employment was not perhaps due to the applicant taking time to care for a dying parent or their cancer-afflicted child? Or perhaps a discarded application was for someone who had a baby and never went back to their employer because they knew they were going to suffer repercussions after taking their full maternity leave.

These are examples of gaps that exist between you seeing them and them being seen. What would it take to get them into the scope of your vision? In a study conducted by Harvard Business School, 90 percent of employers have admitted that their hiring process excludes qualified workers.[8] Yet they raised concern over a lack of skilled workers. Their strategies haven't changed, and their needs remain unmet.

Take notice of the team member who takes notes in the meeting or the eager assistant who crosses his T's and dots his I's. Who are they, and what value are they bringing to their existing role? What potential do they offer? If you discover they are exceeding expectations, perhaps it's time to understand more about this person and what they want to accomplish within (and outside of) the organization.

As mentioned in Chapter 1, in my transition from the Iron Maiden to the Turtle, I began including more personalized attention that went beyond the performance review and into the realm of defining individual purpose. This helped me proactively assess a person's potential for satisfaction and fulfillment within the organization, thus helping me recommend measures to help reduce turnover and increase engagement.

The Unseen Employee may also be the Unseen *Potential* Employee. These are people you have not yet met who are applying to jobs where they have only a 1 percent chance of placement due to impactful information that is not obvious in a cover letter or resume: a forced relocation because of a change in their spouse's career, or unexpected unemployment due to their company's sudden bankruptcy. Maybe they recently immigrated to the country with a specialty that requires them to obtain new credentials or licensing they cannot afford. The same reasons that your existing employees might be unseen could be the same reasons why potential employees don't get asked to interview. Even if they do get the interview, if your evaluation process is based on pattern matching, no matter what they say, they may still not be seen.

Resumes don't speak louder than interviews. Often, quick assumptions are made due to the high volume of applicants. How can you refine your hiring process when you are hiring from both within and outside of the organization? This is likely a great question to ask your chief people officer. Maybe you two can put your heads together and identify the top qualities and skill sets needed for the position, not only for today but for the future, and find those areas in which the company is willing and able to provide training and education.

The Successful Unseen Employee

My first leadership position was as the assistant manager of a shoe store when I was 14 years old. Some of the people reporting to me were upwards of twenty years older. This was the start of me being chosen to lead in really difficult situations, often because of, or I like to think, despite my age. If not because of my age, it was because I was the only female or because I'm part of the LGBTQ+ community, yet I was given the role.

The Unseen Employee might be vocal and driven like I was, or they could be very different in character, perhaps quietly determined and internally motivated. While I can attribute the resilience I had from my childhood to helping me succeed and progress in business, I still experienced not being seen over and over again. The Unseen Employee might have the job or get the promotion and *still* not feel seen. Most often, this is a result of the leader and/or employee not sharing much of themselves, whether it be work and lived experiences, career aspirations, or unique and different skills to be applied.

Are you thinking at this point that you are damned no matter what you do as a leader? I promise you, that's not the idea here. *Awareness* is the idea and the solution that creates understanding. Through awareness, we understand what is happening and who is in the workspace. We become the Turtle. Here, I want to remind you that the Turtle has to make hard decisions, too. You can't be a Turtle if you can't confront the status quo and the things that are not working.

In my youth, I thought I wanted to be a lawyer, but the need to support myself at a young age led me to work at a bank while in university, where I was almost immediately promoted into a leadership role. I thrived—I was continually learning and being challenged. I loved my leadership role, thus affirming my decision that I wanted to stay in the corporate world as a leader.

When I was recruited into a COO role at 24 at a B2B business process outsourcing organization, it was a massive stretch role for me. I was charged with leading all functional areas of the organization except for finance—but I excelled, unknown to me, as the successful Unseen Employee.

Often, I am asked about the role models I had that have inspired me to become the Turtle. And I answered that there were no such Turtles in my life. Don't get me wrong, I have worked for many smart, nice, compassionate people. But were they Turtles? Not one.

In my childhood years, my mom watched a lot of television. With just one television in the house, it meant I watched a lot of her shows, even as a young child of perhaps 8 or 10 years. We watched *Dallas*, the drama series about interfamily conflict among a family of wealthy oil magnates. Watching them, I decided that I wanted to make a lot of money someday. Another show we loved to watch together was *LA Law*, a 1980s legal drama series that influenced my early dream to become a lawyer before I fell in love with leadership.

Even my televised influences weren't Turtles. In both my personal and professional life, I lacked mentors. My mom— an incredible woman who did so much for me—was broken in her own ways. She was later diagnosed with manic depression, making it very difficult to be at home with her. My father, an absent, unemotional, and unaffectionate man, had multiple affairs while married to my mother—he was not a great human and quite poor in all relationships. You see? There was no one to look up to, so I learned to look to myself.

I always had a vision of what my *own* family would one day be like in terms of what I wanted in a partner, my desire to have children, and the kind of healthy relationship dynamics that I wanted but never saw with my own parents. I experienced the same lack of mentorship at work, where I frequently witnessed poor examples of leadership. That didn't stop me from knowing the leader I wanted to become. Seeing who you don't want to be can be incredibly useful in developing yourself as a Whole Human Leader.

Maybe I had a vision because there were a lot of blank spaces that I could fill in. Movies and television helped me do that, but ultimately, I knew I wanted to be happy and successful in my life, so I used my imagination and creativity when there was no one to turn to for guidance.

Relying on myself as a kid, I was always very curious and focused, asking myself a lot of questions. How do I do better? What do I need to learn? Looking back, I get emotional thinking about how the abandonment and disappointment I felt growing up has always been the biggest reason I have wanted to be a person whom my children, my partner, my friends, and my colleagues can count on for help and unwavering support.

I want to be the mentor that I never had.

We all have parts of our lives that play into why we want to become better leaders at work, better humans, in fact. Often, these parts have everything to do with our upbringing and past experiences. The great part about the Turtle is that it uses all of our parts, from both our past and our present, for the betterment of all of us.

The Turtle harnesses the leader in everyone by seeing each individual as a Whole Human Leader. With this attitude, they recognize that there's value in each person and in the team as a whole that goes well beyond the surface.

Unpack your heavy backpack, turning pain points into progress as you do, and lighten your load so you can help others discover that which is hidden inside them, that which contains value and purpose.

Start the process of becoming the Turtle. Yes, it will take time (remember that turtles are patient, and they also keep pace), but rest assured that as you progress you will no longer experience the loneliness and isolation of leadership that you have likely felt in the past.

Emotions are contagious and action provides your team

with clear evidence of your commitment to them. That leads to accountability and trust. This means that being the Turtle *will* resonate with others on the team without you having to say much, if anything, at all. The Turtle *does* because transformation can only take place with action. You don't become the Turtle until you relentlessly and consistently activate all parts of yourself through the conscious practice of Whole Human Leadership.

When we see through our blind spots, we uncover what's possible when it comes to the people around us and our own capacity for empathy and authenticity in leadership. Don't be fooled. Blank is not blind. When there's nothing or no one there, we can fill it with more and more of our vision, including the unseen people who were always there that we somehow failed to notice. Oftentimes that includes ourselves.

Chapter 2 Key Takeaways

○ *The Turtle takes responsibility for the Unseen Employee.*

○ *The Turtle defines success through teamwork.*

○ *The Turtle uses all experiences for the betterment of self and others.*

○ *The Incomplete Leader was often once the Unseen Employee.*

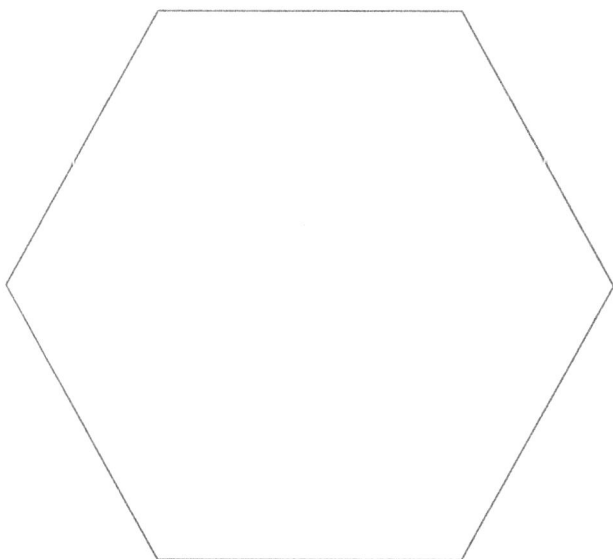

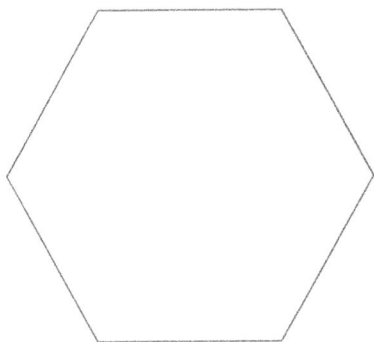

Competencies

for

Performance

"At Apple, as at Google, a boss's ability to achieve results had a lot more to do with listening and seeking to understand than it did with telling people what to do; more to do with debating than directing; more to do with pushing people to decide than with being the decider; more to do with persuading than with giving orders; more to do with learning than with knowing."

— Kim Malone Scott

Radical Candor: Be a Kick-Ass Boss Without Losing Your Humanity

Part **2**

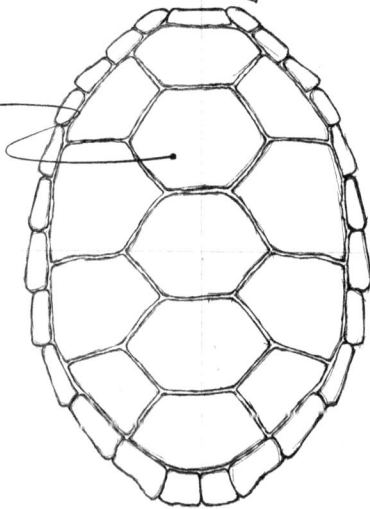

CRITICAL THINKING (CT)

EMOTIONAL
INTELLIGENCE (EI)

Chapter 3

*The Shell and the Body: Critical
Thinking and Emotional Intelligence*

66 Do the right thing." These are
four words I have said to myself
in countless situations, from organizational restructuring to terminating
employees for poor performance to imple-
menting new processes and technologies.

"What is the right thing to do?" A question
that I have had to answer more than I can
count. While there are often clear black-
and-white answers and actions, I have
found myself in grey zones just as often, if
not more frequently.

As the Iron Maiden, I had yet to carve
out *all* of my core values because my focus
was more heavily directed toward meeting
business expectations and outcomes, and
I was young and still maturing. When I
found myself in a grey zone, I deferred to
my role, the rules, and the leader because
I was still defining my core values. It's
important to point out, however, that as the

Iron Maiden, I was always clear on what was right and wrong, moral or immoral, ethical and unethical.

When I discovered fraud during my tenure at my first C-suite position, I informed the CEO. The company's co-founder, a client, and two of my employees were at the helm of the fraud. I took the necessary step of terminating the employees involved. However, when the CEO expressed his unwillingness to either dismiss or buy out the cofounder, allowing that individual to remain in a leadership position within the company, I made the decision to resign. There was no way I would associate myself with an unethical person who held such a prominent public image within our company.

While I decided to leave rather quickly, feeling disappointed and discouraged, I did not display any emotional outbursts. Doing so would have been unprofessional, but more than that, I would have created unnecessary sparks that could ultimately have spread a wildfire of negative emotions that would disrupt the team.

Following that experience, I gained greater confidence and a clearer sense of my core values. I also became more proactive in assessing the individuals I collaborated with and the organizations I served. In my subsequent departures, I embodied the Turtle and provided highly detailed explanations for my resignations that were rooted in values and, often, ethical and moral considerations.

Every leader, including you, will have their process for determining the right thing and what to do about it, but there are universal lessons that need to be understood. To begin, it's important to explain the two foundational parts of the Turtle: critical thinking (CT) and emotional intelligence (EI). To think critically is to objectively analyze and evaluate an issue or situation without judgment in order to form a conclusion that is justified through the analysis rather than by your opinion or through an anecdotal experience.[9] To be emotionally intelligent is to be aware of the emotions of yourself and others, to be able to regulate your own emotions and handle interpersonal relations judiciously and empathetically. While CT is of the head and EI is of the heart, they are both vital to Whole Human Leadership, and the connection they have to one another is well worth examining.

Mitigating Emotional Contagion through Critical Thinking and Emotional Intelligence

Keeping pace as the Turtle is not only an action-based practice, it is a practice in thought. When we rush our thoughts, we run the risk of igniting that wildfire I mentioned earlier. Emotional contagion is a form of social influence that involves the spread of emotions and related behaviours. As a leader, I realize it is particularly important that I carry this awareness with me and maintain an understanding that my energy has a profound impact on those around me. Leadership is a serious responsibility, and we cannot afford to be plagued with rampant flames popping up because of our inability to process our thoughts and emotions.

Self-awareness and self-reflection have been invaluable tools for me, as they shift my focus away from external factors and give me the opportunity to focus on my own priorities. By taking the time to explore the reasons behind my own emotional responses, I've been able to identify actions, language, and behaviours that I can adjust to move forward in a more positive direction.

In the absence of CT and EI, we often react impulsively, which is less than ideal in the business world, as well as in our personal lives. By embracing CT and EI, we can refine our intuitive responses, acting from a place of confidence and understanding rather than mere reactivity.[10] I refer to this as "gut intuition," as instinct remains unchangeable while intuition can be cultivated. How can you tell if you're reacting impulsively? You might experience symptoms stemming from unregulated emotions, such as trembling hands or that heart-thumping sensation in your throat during tense moments. You might second-guess yourself or spend sleepless nights questioning your decisions.

A Whole Human Leader recognizes that approaching situations with mindfulness and emotional awareness fosters sustainable and meaningful relationships. Remaining attuned and composed, even in chaotic environments, enhances my ability to comprehend what others may be thinking or feeling based on their reactions and expressions. It allows me to really hear them.

In my personal life, I find pleasure in quietly observing interactions at a restaurant, such as between diners and the service staff. It's fascinating to witness how a guest's complaint, for instance, can be delivered either in frustration or in a calm and collected manner and the impact it has on the server's or manager's demeanor before and after the interaction. I don't know about you, but when I dine at my favourite restaurants, I want the staff to serve me with a high level of care. In my experience, you have to give care to receive it in return. This shift can elevate your team from simply "doing their job" to going above and beyond their role requirements.

The protective shell and inner core of the Turtle, represented respectively by CT and EI, empower you and your team to navigate uncertainty, generate innovative ideas, confidently overcome challenges, and eliminate unnecessary stressors.

Reflecting on my earlier career, I can admit to experiencing a few setbacks when it came to building lasting relationships in the workplace. However, there is one notable triumph that readily comes to mind.

Due to my diverse roles and involvement in numerous merger and acquisition transactions, I have often found myself leading integration and restructuring activities. One such instance was the acquisition of a corporate travel company, an industry I was relatively new to. Initially, I was hired by the parent company to oversee their shared services organization. Over time, my role evolved to include ending a joint venture, orchestrating corporate rebranding, navigating an IPO, and overseeing the acquisition of six companies, all within a relatively short time frame. As a result of these acquisitions and the establishment of a new headquarters in New York City, I was relocated to the United States to lead North American operations.

There I was, arriving in New York City at the age of 30, hailing from Toronto, with only a year and a half of experience in the travel industry. Immediately, I found myself surrounded by formidable New Yorkers who questioned my credentials as a young woman with limited travel industry knowledge. A significant aspect of the acquisition and integration involved meeting with key clients to understand their programs and needs so I could project confidence and stability in our future partnership. Additionally, I needed to invest considerable time with my team, both as a collective unit and through one-on-one interactions with each direct report. This allowed me to gain insights into their backgrounds, experiences, and teams, as well as the clients they served.

It was during this period that I encountered Kate, a resilient 60-year-old New Yorker responsible for managing one of the most prominent clients acquired through the merger. Upon our first encounter, her gaze seemed to convey skepticism, as if she were thinking, "Who is this woman half my age, now in a leadership position, shaping our business strategy, giving me directives, and yet unfamiliar with the intricacies of our industry?" It took nearly a year of consistent effort to earn her trust.

My time investment in Kate was well worth the effort. Whole Human Leadership requires knowing that you cannot rush trust and you can't escape the challengers, those people who feel like predators waiting to swallow you whole through their speed. Remember, the Turtle sets the pace.

The shell of a turtle becomes thicker over time, a sign of increased resilience. Yours will, too. In due course, after I took the time needed to actively listen and process what Kate had said, reflect on my experiences with her, and consider her experiences and how they might have influenced her thoughts and feelings, I felt ready to create a strategic plan of intentional actions that would serve as the foundation for developing trust between us. My very first act was to set up a meeting with Kate, where I verbally recognized her talents and experience so she understood that I knew the value she created on the team. I referred to her strengths, signalling to her that I was not going to overshadow her capabilities or undermine her wisdom and know-how.

Going through this process strengthened my confidence by acting courageously (not to be overly dramatic, but I definitely felt some fear and anxiety in working to get on Kate's good side). Courage is a contagious emotion that bred confidence in me, resulting in Kate finding the courage of her own and overcoming her own fears by deciding to trust me as a leader.

The Connection Between CT and EI

There's a deliberate reason why CT is positioned before EI in this chapter. While the most adept critical thinkers can approach problems with a detached, scientific mindset, the majority of us struggle to completely remove emotional bias from the equation. I personally find that critical thinking helps alert me to any rising emotions I may be experiencing. And this is a necessary first step to objectively assessing the situation.

My relationship with Kate exemplified an interpersonal scenario where I needed to temporarily set my emotions aside and apply logical reasoning as the first step to coming forth as a Whole Human Leader. Please don't be mistaken, I wasn't denying my emotions. Instead, I was creating space to process them before I responded. Doing so allowed me to regulate my emotions while simultaneously avoiding a potential relationship-damaging reaction. Hitting pause on my emotions provided space to think critically so I could first consider how Kate's lived experiences could potentially be impacting the way she was receiving me. From there I was able to intelligently work with my emotions, recognizing the potentially sensitive nature of interacting with Kate. With tact and strategic attention, this process allowed me to converse with her in a calm voice, even in moments when I sensed she was tense or skeptical.

Here's the crux of the matter: we require self-regulation (EI) to engage in critical thinking, and simultaneously, thinking critically aids us in self-regulation by creating space from emotions to focus on the facts. It is this synergy between the two modes that allows us to be fully prepared to engage in any situation with any person.

A leader who doesn't practice the synergy of CT and EI is not a complete Turtle. To embody the Turtle, one must not only comprehend but also actively employ both CT and EI. Later, we will explore when to emphasize one over the other, but in the realm of Whole Human Leadership, there's never a complete absence of either CT or EI. All facets of the Turtle must come into play in order to project stability and balance to your team and to prevent the disconnection from them that can possibly happen due to inconsistent behaviour on your part. If you swing back and forth to extremes on the pendulum, the likelihood of you being misunderstood increases. More than likely, you *will* make this mistake, but with increased self-awareness, you can work toward finding that sweet seat of integration that hovers around the centre of the pendulum.

Here's an example. When it's time to review your financial statements, do you ever get a surge of apprehension just before examining the reports? But then you find that once you delve into the facts and figures, you can set aside the initial anxiety because your critical thinking skills have swung into action, analyzed and made sense of the results, and calmed your nerves. Whether you find the results favourable or not, you experience a sense of emotional regulation because you have the facts at your disposal. Emotions still exist, but having gathered the facts, you can now calmly formulate a strategic plan for moving forward.

Approaching matters solely from an analytical or emotional standpoint leaves us incomplete, as it fails to provide a holistic understanding of the entire situation.

In summary, CT and EI are two indispensable skills that synergize to guide us in making informed decisions.

What Benefits Result From Integrating CT And EI?

Improved decision-making: *CT skills help us to evaluate information and make sound decisions, while EI skills help us to consider the emotional impact of our decisions.*

Increased creativity: *CT skills help us to generate new ideas and solve problems creatively, while EI skills help us to collaborate effectively with others and build a supportive environment for creativity.*

Enhanced leadership: *CT skills help us to make sound decisions and solve problems effectively, while EI skills help us to build relationships and motivate others.*

Reduced stress: *CT skills help us to manage our emotions and cope with difficult situations effectively, while EI skills help us to build resilience and maintain a positive outlook.*

The Shell: Critical Thinking

The fact that Kate had significant industry experience and knowledge that I did not and that I had a very different experience and skill set to bring to the table was crucial to developing trust between us.

Enter the logic of the Turtle shell.

Fact: Kate was from New York, a culture that appreciates direct communication.

I decided to tell her what I thought, and I was confident in telling her because all of what I said was indisputable. "Kate, there are a lot of things I don't know, and this is where the two of us complement one another. You've got this incredibly deep expertise, and the client loves you. But here's what I can bring to the table..." Now, this didn't win her over right away, but we made progress. She began engaging with me more often.

When faced with difficult decisions or uncomfortable situations, we can use our CT skills to weigh the pros and cons of each option and to make the best decision possible. Just as a turtle uses its shell to protect itself from danger, we can use CT to protect ourselves from making bad decisions or reacting in a way that leads to remorse. I am using Kate's story because we often don't consider that these types of interpersonal relationship dynamics require not just EI but CT to regulate our emotions to help us become empathetic.

The shell protects, strengthens, adapts, and sustains. Working with Kate became one of the most transformative moments in relationship-building of my early career and gave me more wisdom in knowing that there are always facts that can help us bridge gaps.

<hr />

Skills to Develop Critical Thinking

<hr />

Squarely face difficult choices: *When faced with challenging decisions that fall under your responsibilities, confront them head-on to gain valuable experience. If you're uneasy, acknowledge the unfamiliarity of the situation. And if you ever find yourself at a crossroads, don't hesitate to reach out to a trusted and respected colleague for guidance.*

Go beyond personal perspectives: *Push yourself to explore and understand viewpoints outside your own realm of experience. This can lead to valuable insights that strengthen your ability to analyze situations.*

Welcome candid critiques: *Regularly seek out genuine feedback as a tool for self-improvement. View it objectively as constructive input for growth, not as a personal affront.*

—————◇—————

Practice Makes the Turtle

—————◇—————

Quick Questions: Critical Thinking

If you can answer YES to *all* of these questions, you have the critical thinking skills of the Turtle:

Am I setting goals for the team that reflect the needs of all stakeholders, including employees, customers, and shareholders?

Did I take the time to gather information from a variety of reliable sources and weigh the pros and cons before making a decision?

Am I receiving honest feedback when I ask for it? Have I set up trust with the team, so they feel confident in safely providing direct feedback to me?

The last time I facilitated a conflict between employees, did I remain objective and fair by listening to both sides to find a solution that works for everyone and is in line with our goals?

Do I encourage the participation and sharing of ideas often and do I allow others space to talk, share their perspective, and change their mind?

The Body: Emotional Intelligence

How did I become the Turtle? Through consistently taking incremental steps and practicing the things that made me uncomfortable. Over time, I got better at articulating my emotions at work. Often, as a leader, you'll find yourself stuck in the very centre of an issue. By using critical thinking to assess the situation based on facts and to discern the effective from the ineffective, you can retain a composed demeanor during tense moments. When you revisit your feelings, identify your emotions, and manage them to your advantage and to the success of everyone around you through EI, you communicate with renewed empathy and understanding. You will steadily improve as you continue your journey to becoming the Turtle. I had to neutralize Kate's reaction toward me to shift the dynamic between us.

"I'm going to support you with our transition in this business, Kate. I've got your back. I am here to help." These were the last words I spoke to Kate before we were blindsided by a massive delivery issue for one of our clients in her portfolio. An emergency senior leadership meeting was called. Kate was present. When asked who caused the issue, I spoke up. "It doesn't matter *who* made the error. I am accountable for this team. I don't need to name names. A conversation has been had with the person who made the error, and there's a development plan in place for them." Out of the corner of my eye, I saw Kate's shoulders soften. I turned my head toward her and noticed that the corners of her mouth were slightly turned up. Coming from her, a tough New Yorker, I knew this was a pivotal moment in our relationship.

Skills to Develop Emotional Intelligence

Reflect before responding: In heated moments, give yourself a momentary break, be it a single breath or a minute, before you answer. Cultivate a habit of informing those around you that you'll respond after some reflection.

Prioritize others' emotions: Foster empathetic conversations by tuning into the potential emotions of the other person. For clarity, inquire directly if they are experiencing those feelings.

Body language: Observe body language and facial cues, and moderate your approach if tension seems evident.

Practice Makes the Turtle

Quick Questions: Emotional Intelligence

If you can answer YES to *all* of these questions, you have the Emotional Intelligence skills of the Turtle:

When giving feedback or working through a conflict, do I avoid making personal attacks or blaming employees?

Before, during, and after conflict resolution, am I objective and fair in my assessment?

○ *Before starting a meeting, do I take a few minutes to "read the room"?*

○ *Do I regularly seek the viewpoints of colleagues and staff instead of making assumptions?*

○ *When deciding, do I consider the emotional ramifications for all stakeholders and determine if my choice aligns with their well-being?*

———————◇———————

How to Know When to Use CT Versus When to Use EI

———————◇———————

I'd like to impart some hard-earned wisdom about how to learn to trust yourself and how to practice and fail successfully (which we will address in more depth in Part 5). Every situation is different, but a general rule of thumb, based upon my own experience, is that when it comes to issues related to finance, process, and procedure, lean on CT. When it comes to relationships, DEI, transformation, and change management, lean on EI.

When faced with a difficult situation, an emotionally intelligent leader will be able to remain under control by using what I call strategic intentionality. Develop a plan, mobilize, and utilize a high degree of EI to be successful. Using their shells to protect themselves from predators, an emotionally intelligent leader uses their EI to protect the confidence of their team members, cut the drama, and solve problems with creativity and compassion.

The Turtle employs a dynamic blend of CT and EI to build intentional relationships. The reason I wanted Kate and me to have a strong relationship was not only about the business. I wanted to build rapport and a relationship with her authentically and collaborate with her. Kate was fiercely admired in the industry, and I wanted to gain more insight into the business sector through her. In other words, I was quite intentional about building my relationship with her.

Deliberately fostering a relationship is a strategic endeavour, as it demands dedication to navigate conflicts and hurdles. Ultimately, the goal is to emerge with enhanced mutual understanding and collaboration. When I met Kate, I was beginning my transition to the Turtle, so practicing with her was vital for my growth and hers. I'm not sure if Kate viewed it that way, but I like to think that she took something out of that year that I practiced patience, kept my cool, stood my ground, and gained her trust. The Turtle doesn't expect other people to grow but rather grows because there's a desire to become better and a belief that if they model Whole Human Leadership, the right people will surround them.

My experience with Kate was a huge success. After a year of building trust with her, she became one of the voices most supportive of my leadership with the senior people who had spent over twenty years working at the company we acquired. She got on board, and they followed. How did I know that I had finally won Kate over? She spoke up in a team meeting that was held to discuss more changes that needed to be made. We had acquired another company, so I was going to have to do more restructuring, and she was an advocate for me among other voices of dissension at the table. At that moment, the Turtle inside me smiled and thought, "Okay, all of this work is paying off."

Chapter 3 Key Takeaways

- *Both critical thinking and emotional intelligence are skills that can be refined and improved. There are moments to prioritize CT and others to emphasize EI.*

- *Use critical thinking and emotional intelligence to motivate your team. Stay compassionate during periods of dissension and conflict among the team.*

- *Being strategically intentional requires a blend of tactical planning and genuine empathy.*

- *Value understanding the perspectives and experiences of others.*

- *Without taking steps forward, no change occurs.*

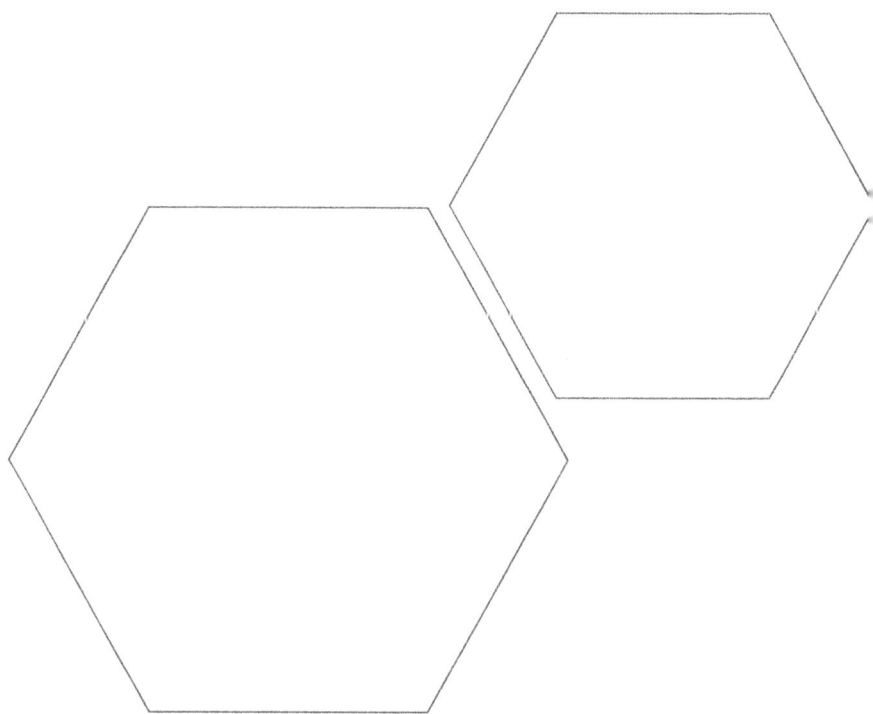

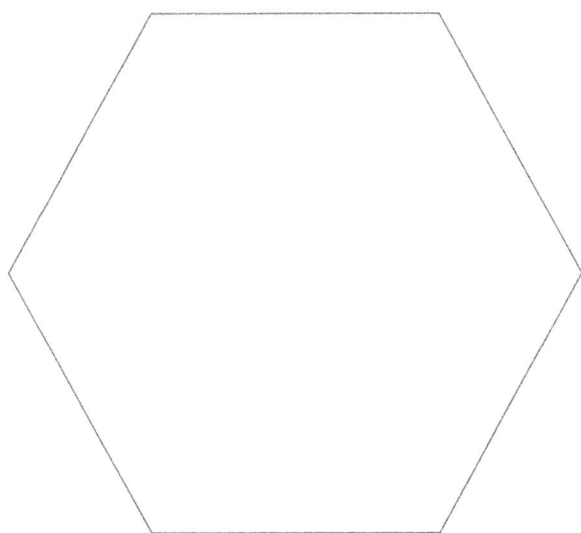

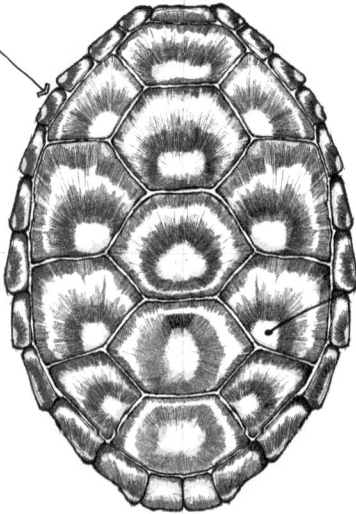

AUTHENTICITY

EMPATHY

Chapter 4

The Head and The Heart:
Leading with Empathy and Authenticity

Within only a few months of hiring John as an executive partner, I was confident that I had made a mistake. John came well-recommended and with an impressive resume. But sometimes resumes and interviews don't provide the full accounting of how a person really is. John felt the need to ensure that every member of the team, regardless of rank or career accolades, was aware of his executive position and status. Whether out of insecurity or a need to bully others, he consistently used his title and authority to grandstand and enforce hierarchy in the team. When challenged by others, especially when concerning a strategic plan for client solutions or something related to pricing, his retort would be to exclaim, "I'm the Partner here. What I say goes." To John, this statement was a convincing conversation-ender. He gave his own opinions and ideas more weight than those of others and was quick to shut down discussions with those who had contrasting views.As a result, he soon lost buy-in from his colleagues.

Many on the team avoided him or talked negatively about him behind his back. Those who did speak to him were often insulted by his overt attempts to take credit for work that either they or others on the team had produced.

Fortunately, at this point in my career, I was operating fully as the Turtle. I was at ease being forthright, compassionate, and open about my feelings. I had consistently trained myself to inquire instead of making assumptions, enabling me to genuinely grasp, directly from my team members, their emotions and thoughts. This level of intimate communication made it easier to address problems and drive meaningful change.

As a Turtle, I usually resort to curiosity when things get sticky. This seemed like the right approach to take with John. I wanted to figure out where his behaviour was coming from. If I could do that, I could then work to coach him into developing a more positive communication style for the good of the team. One day, after yet another uncomfortable meeting with a team member who brought his behaviour to my attention, I asked John if we could sit down together for a video call.

"John, I'm receiving feedback from a multitude of places, including your peers and direct reports. I want to share with you what I am hearing," His lips pursed as I spoke. This was an obvious clue to me that he was trying not to get outwardly upset. So, I pulled back and decided that this would be a great time to share my own experience as a leader with him.

I told him about my previous Iron Maiden-like tendencies, describing my inability to fully connect with my teams years before. I explained how I had discovered that a large part of this came from my fears and insecurity about my experience level and my differences compared to my peers.

As I spoke, I waited for a sign that he was internalizing my story and how it related to his current situation. I suspected that he was as insecure as I had once been, whether about himself or about being a new person joining our established organization.

"I was frightened to show any side of myself personally, to show vulnerability," I continued. I asked him to ruminate over the next several days about our conversation and the feedback I had provided before we regrouped and discussed the next steps.

I also specifically asked him not to react immediately or reach out to any of the team members. I can recall him looking down at the computer screen toward his lap. Since we were on a video call, I couldn't see what he was doing or get a better read on his body language.

It was a Friday, so I thought it an opportune time for him to take a few days to consider everything we discussed before taking steps to change. I ended our call by scheduling our follow-up discussion and committing to working together to navigate the situation with the other people involved. He agreed. "The next time we meet," I told him with a sincere and supportive tone of voice, "we can talk about how you can start to show up differently."

Shortly after our call, my phone was blowing up, starting with one of his direct reports, who he had messaged during our video call and again directly after we ended the meeting. He was targeting his direct reports, blaming them, and accusing them of going to me rather than him. John didn't internalize what I had shared with him. Likely, the only voice he heard during the meeting was the one that was telling him he had been wronged. He didn't want to relate or connect. He wanted to play a role and he was not ready or equipped to be a Whole Human Leader at that time.

Unfortunately, like so many other Incomplete Leaders, years later, John still proudly broadcasts his role as "Partner," and his colleagues continue to complain about him behind his back. I had hoped to continue to coach and develop him or manage him out of the business if it was necessary, but I left the organization to pursue another opportunity within a couple of months of this conversation.

While the odds are that you will experience many wins during the long game with Whole Human Leadership, there will be times when the empathy and authenticity you lead with will not produce the outward impact you are looking for. If you let the Johns of the world deter you, you have yet to transform into the Turtle. All that means is that you get to keep practicing.

The Connection Between Empathy and Authenticity

Empathy is the ability to understand and share the feelings of another person, often drawing from your own relatable experiences. Authenticity is being true to yourself and your values, beliefs, and identity. Here our previously discussed tools of emotional intelligence and critical thinking come into play again as being the precursor skills that enable you to effectively connect with your team with real empathy and authenticity.

Before we explore the connection between authenticity and empathy, it's important to acknowledge their distinctions. The former has nothing to do with other people. It's an inside job of reducing the amount of tension between how you feel and how you act so you can operate in the world with a higher level of empathy. The way this works is that both authenticity and empathy are give-and-take exchanges. There's a feedback loop between them. While they may not be actualized at the same time, it is likely that as you become more keenly aware of one, the other will begin to be more apparent. Vulnerability is present in both authenticity and empathy.[11] Being honest about who we are and accessing and sharing personal moments that others can relate to requires us to be vulnerable.

If I had used the Iron Maiden approach with John and left my vulnerability at the door, that conversation would have been in-complete for me. Here's why. My own vulnerability showed me a lot about John's capacity. He was not, and may not ever be, ready, willing, or able to have those types of conversations. If I had stayed at the company, I would have engaged in a long-term con-versation with John that would have helped us develop a perfor-mance plan for him, something that balanced his performance and ability to think critically with his level of emotional intelli-gence.

John was clearly driven by strong emotions, made evident through his struggle to accept feedback, his tendency to imme-diately reach out to others, and his failure to give himself time to reflect on the situation and grow from it. If John were the Turtle, he would have thoughtfully and empathetically taken into account the feelings and concerns expressed by his team members instead of hastily defending himself and responding negatively.

Had I presented myself as the Iron Maiden, devoid of self-awareness, I might not have connected with and compre-hended John as deeply as I did, potentially leaving me perplexed by his behaviour. While I believe retaining someone like John for an extended period solely to help him improve as a person can be detrimental and foster a toxic environment, I can still empathize with him. In this instance, my empathy wasn't something he ap-preciated or gleaned anything helpful from. Yet, extending that compassion was advantageous for me.

With my genuine and compassionate approach, I found peace of mind and freed myself from doubts and regrets. I hope you can experience the same. Sticking to the Iron Maiden persona was challenging, just as embodying the Turtle is. However, becoming the latter has enabled me to show the world my authentic self, true to my own experience, with all my strengths and vulnerabilities. It has also helped me to become far more empathetic to others and to understand people better, such as John. The connection between authenticity and empathy becomes clear in moments like these.

The Heart: Empathy

Whether you succeed or falter, triumph or fall short, cultivating empathy is a journey, as it fundamentally revolves around striving to acquire a deeper understanding and reaching the essence of an individual or circumstance. Embracing curiosity is the key to fostering empathy because curiosity is what provides the motivation to probe for answers, to grasp the hoped-for goal of having a clear, unobstructed view of the other person.

With John, I took the time and set aside moments to try to truly comprehend his perspective. This provided me with valuable insights that were crucial for strategic intention. When plotting a course and taking action, it's vital to ascertain whether you're on the path toward your desired destination or are heading straight into a cul-de-sac.

Curiosity shouldn't be mistaken for prying when collecting information. For true empathy, it's crucial to approach situations with a balance of analytical thinking (CT) and a genuine sense of discovery (embracing the unknown). Without this balance, biases or preconceived notions could hinder your empathetic journey. Empathy demands a suspension of judgment, or at the very least, the capability to set aside biases, enabling genuine and attentive listening. By fostering this genuine curiosity and sidelining any prejudgements, you pave the way to the most rewarding phase: forming authentic connections.

The Turtle knows how to be empathetic without sacrificing core values. If John explained to me that he was, in fact, insecure in himself or his new role, I would have understood where his behaviour was coming from (although it would still not serve as a justification for his language or conduct).

It's important to note that it isn't effective or appropriate to counter or label John as "wrong"; doing so could diminish his feelings or the experiences driving his actions. Engaging with genuine curiosity, transparency, impartiality, and empathy fosters an environment conducive to understanding, admitting mistakes, or embracing alternative perspectives.[12] It treads very lightly when it comes to judging people or their actions as "right" or "wrong."

Alerting a team member when they receive negative feedback, violate a policy, or overstep a boundary is crucial in Whole Human Leadership. Regarding John, if there's an absence of willingness from him coupled with tacit approval or indifference from the leadership, it's natural that certain members of the team might experience feelings of disillusionment or disappointment. Fortunately, a Whole Human Leader can successfully manage such situations with their integrity unscathed.

Skill to Develop Empathy

Start with yourself: *Write about your day, emphasizing the emotions you remember feeling. Did you experience empathy from others at any point in your day? Did you exhibit empathy toward a colleague?*

Recognize others: *Who did you interact with today? Pick one of those people and write about what you think their day was like based on your interactions with them. Remember to note their body language, tone of voice, and what they told you to help inform your journaling.*

Ask great questions: *Brainstorm and come up with three open-ended questions that you could ask others to help yourself understand more about what they might be feeling. After you come up with these questions, start asking and see what you learn!*

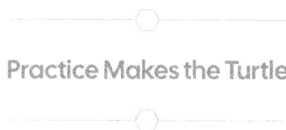

Practice Makes the Turtle

Quick Questions: Empathy

If you can answer YES to *all* of these questions, you have the empathy of the Turtle:

○ *During team meetings, do I ensure a distraction-free environment? Do I emphasize my dedication and presence by notifying colleagues in advance of possible interruptions?*

○ *Do I practice patience by letting someone complete their thoughts before responding, aiming for this at least 80 percent of the time?*

○ *Is it common for me to pose in-depth, open-ended queries to my team, clients, and peers?*

○ *Am I always attuned to nonverbal signals like gestures, facial reactions, and vocal tones to gauge someone's emotions?*

When someone faces challenges, do I step forward to provide support and reassure them of my concern?

Do I consistently acknowledge and applaud the accomplishments of both the entire team and its individual members?

The Head: Authenticity

Being authentic means aligning your actions with your words, regardless of the situation or context.

When I am at the gym, you might find me wearing tank tops that *I* like to think are funny (my friends and colleagues may offer differing opinions). My sense of humour shows up through the sayings written on them, some of which have expletives. This, however, is not the sense of humour I wear on display at the office. We're not talking about presenting two different versions of Victoria and her sense of humour. We're talking about presenting different expressions of the same personality for different contexts, environments, and audiences. Context matters. I'm not afraid if someone takes an "awkward" photo. I'll post it myself. However, maybe it's not the most appropriate thing for a client to see me wearing a shirt with a swear word on it. But it's still all me.

In opening up about my own life, I have had to ask myself what parts of my story make sense and are most meaningful to share.

My answer: any part that will remove a barrier to progress.

I'm convinced that we cannot truly disentangle ourselves from our personal experiences, and attempting to do so is detrimental. Consider the metaphorical backpack we carry, filled with stress and traumatic memories, thinking its weight is invisible to others. If we don't process and unpack its contents, it can lead to leadership styles reminiscent of the Iron Maiden. However, when we unpack the contents, we might discover valuable things like connection, insight, belonging, and self-assuredness, now viewed with a fresh perspective. Sharing these experiences can be a potent tool to turn them into beneficial insights.

For instance, if I begin a meeting by letting you know I'm facing challenges with my teenager, it can shed light on why I might seem distant or less communicative. Instead of leaving room for speculation, I believe in being straightforward and sincere. This is the essence of being authentic.

In the majority of tough circumstances, staying true to oneself ensures you're on the right path. Reflecting on some of the hardest discussions I've led makes my heart heavy. Yet, I take pride in having had the courage to face these trying situations. When guiding emerging leaders, many confess their apprehensions about initiating difficult conversations. I emphasize that leadership isn't a fit for everyone. Embracing the role of a Whole Human Leader means frequently confronting discomfort until it becomes second nature.

Incomplete Leadership will leave you feeling like there was more you could have done. You won't feel this sense of unfinished business when you grow into becoming an authentic Whole Human Leader.

Skills to Develop Authenticity

Dedicate time to introspection: *What drives you? What kind of leader do you want to be? Ponder your strengths, areas of improvement, values, and purpose.*

Prioritize transparent communication: *Share your thought process, emotions, and choices with your team. Relay your aspirations for the group and remain receptive to their input.*

Be vulnerable: *Let your team see your humanity. Discuss your missteps and learning experiences. After you come up with them, start asking and see what you learn!*

―――――◇―――――

Practice Makes the Turtle

―――――◇―――――

Quick Questions: Authenticity

If you can answer YES to *all* of these questions, you are showing up authentically like the Turtle:

○ *Have I dedicated time to understanding my strengths, areas for improvement, and communication style?*

○ *Do I openly convey my thoughts and emotions to my team, even in challenging situations?*

○ *If someone observed my conduct across various life scenarios, would they witness consistency aligned with my values?*

○ *Can I acknowledge my errors with assurance?*

○ *Am I at ease admitting my lack of knowledge on a subject? Am I comfortable stating "I don't know"?*

Do I have a mentor whose genuine nature I respect and who offers me valuable guidance and support?

How Much Empathy and Authenticity Does It Take to Become the Turtle?

There's no clear answer to this question other than to give it your all! Train yourself relentlessly until Whole Human Leadership becomes your default mode of leadership in both your professional and personal life.

It's interesting to consider how much to expose yourself on this journey because a big part of being a Whole Human Leader is demonstrating a degree of vulnerability. When I told my colleague that I cried at the movie theatre way back when that was me unknowingly being vulnerable and authentic. I realized now, that she was given a piece of information about me that likely changed her judgement of my character positively. What about maintaining appropriate boundaries at work? What's the right balance between showing your humanity and vulnerability while creating a culture of no excuses and great accountability?

I think you have to go about it with a strategic mindset. My rule of thumb is that everything I share is geared toward fostering greater connection and understanding and progressing the team's performance. Acting on behalf of the company's mission and the individual and collective purpose of the team is what makes sense to me at work. If I am using empathy and authenticity to build rapport and, ultimately, trust to increase understanding and reduce unnecessary friction, I feel like I am on the right track. If, like in the case of John, your plan fails, you'll suffer disruption and slow progress, but you will be able to overcome such setbacks. Rest assured, as the Turtle, you will become great at making choices that sustain your Whole Human Leadership mentality no matter what comes your way.

Chapter 4 Key Takeaways

- *Grasping empathy and authenticity becomes simpler when you're familiar with CT and EI.*

- *As you hone your empathy and authenticity skills, your relationships will become deeper and more resilient. Leading with empathy and authenticity helps soften feelings of disappointment or conflict.*

- *With empathy and authenticity, even the toughest dialogues will offer clear insights into the subsequent actions you should take, regardless of the result.*

- *Being the Turtle makes hard conversations feel easier.*

- *Empathy and authenticity are best practiced together.*

- *Employ boundaries when opening up.*

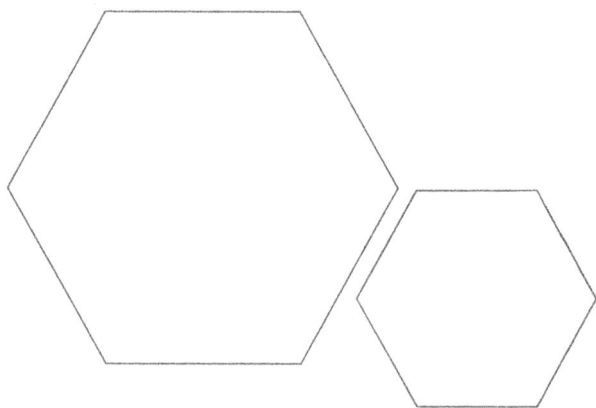

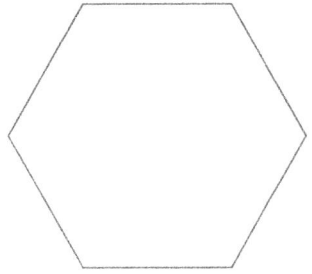

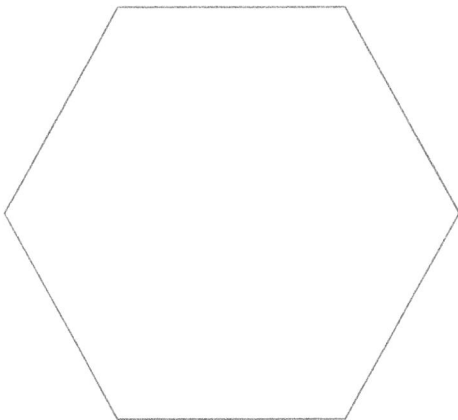

Competencies

for

Sustainable

Success

"As for us, those who choose to embrace the infinite mindset, our journey will lead us to feel inspired every morning, safe when we are working, and fulfilled at the end of each day. And when it's time to leave the game, we will look back at our lives and our careers and say, 'I lived a life worth living and important when imagining what the future holds. We will see how many people we've inspired to carry on the journey without us.'"

— **Simon Sinek**

The Infinite Game

Part **3**

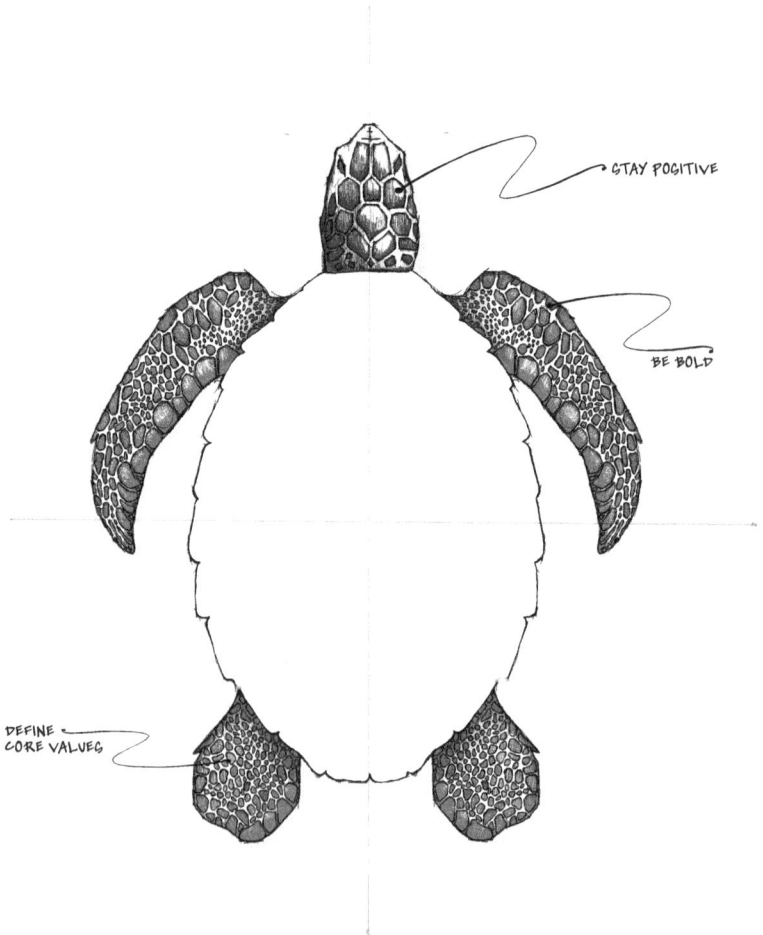

STAY POSITIVE

BE BOLD

DEFINE
CORE VALUES

Chapter 5

Navigating Change with Authenticity

" Tim, this death by a thousand cuts has to stop." I sat in front of the North American President of the company I worked for, looking at him skeptically. We had completed six acquisitions in eighteen months, often laying off hundreds of people at a time. Understandably, an overwhelming sense of fear and anxiety resonated throughout the company. I felt the tension rise every time we declared more layoffs.

A critical part of successful change management is open dialogue: providing context, transparency, and accountability in decision-making. I couldn't stand in front of my team and tell them they were safe. I didn't *know* if they were safe. The incremental cuts continued, on and on, and morale was sinking. The situation would have been much different if only we had instead taken decisive, bold action to make the difficult organizational changes necessary for sustained long-term success.

The incremental, short-term focused, cost-cutting measures were not helping anyone be productive or move forward in support of our mission. Our change management strategy was taking an emotional and mental toll on our employees. If I were to describe the culture at that point, I would call it panic-stricken.

I thought about what would be going through my mind if I were in their place. More than likely, they were spending time looking for new jobs, nursing their distress at home to the detriment of their personal lives, and preoccupied with whether they were going to lose their jobs.

And the issue went beyond the fact that we were negatively impacting the livelihoods of our employees: as leaders, we were not making the courageous decisions to set the business up for mid-to-long-term success. Instead of building the right structures and aligning the right people into those roles, we were building a structure around certain people who seemed "protected," or who Tim was afraid to take action against. The golf course memberships, NBA box suites, and other luxurious expenditures of the executives made it to my P&L reports, so I knew what was going on. Spending in surplus on such things, as we were slashing jobs, was inappropriate in my opinion.

The Whole Human Leader in me needed to fight for change. Given that I was someone in a client-facing position who had spent over 220 days on the road that year, and that I led a majority of the operational delivery teams of employees, I had to be the one to put my foot down. I didn't leave my young children at home to compromise my ethics and values to support actions that I believed were to the detriment of the company.

I needed to do something about the situation, so I went to Tim to ask him to press the STOP button on the horrible slash-and-burn tactics. I expected that I would be shut down, but there was no way I would keep doing this. Eighty percent of the North American headcount of the company was my responsibility—as their leader, I couldn't let them continue to suffer in this way.

"Be bold or go home," I told myself before I sat down with him. A few weeks earlier, before what was to be the final round of layoffs I would carry out, I had looked the other members of leadership in the face and assured them that it would be the last time I would be involved.

Unsurprisingly, during our meeting, Tim didn't back my position or explore other options. Up until that point, I had not viewed him as a strong leader; however, at this juncture, I completely lost respect for him.

Well, I was bold. And in the end, I decided to go home.

I recalled another nickname that I had been given back at some point in my career that I have yet to mention: the Turn-around Queen. This originally referred to my ability to increase performance and engagement. But the situation with Tim gave it a whole new meaning.

I know when to go. And that is when my job is complete.

Working with Tim, I did everything that I could do to help the company with the acquisitions and integrations before my departure. When I was finished, I turned around, faced my purpose, and moved forward to help another organization that needed me.

Leadership is not attached to a job or a position. It belongs to you.

Navigating Change: The Turtle's Approach

A turtle spends most of its time in the water. Like life, the water is unpredictable. We have to learn how to swim both through and around the unexpected to not only survive, but thrive.

Skillfully navigating change means becoming more adaptable and developing the ability to swiftly manoeuvre around obstacles, which often appear without warning. It means that you sometimes have to stick your neck out! The courage I have had in making hard decisions—which were not always popular but provided valuable learning experiences—demonstrates how to show up as a Whole Human Leader. For the Turtle, doing what you think is right for your stakeholders is a huge part of navigating change.

Adapting to change is an essential life skill, given that change is a constant in both the personal and professional spheres. People can utilize a variety of strategies and methods to cope with and thrive amidst change. For example:

- **Acceptance:** *The first step in adapting to any change is acknowledging and accepting it. This doesn't necessarily mean liking it, but recognizing that it's a reality.*

- **Stay positive:** *A positive mindset can help one see the opportunities that come with change rather than focusing solely on what has been lost or altered.*

- **Be proactive:** *Instead of being passive, take active steps to learn about the change, and see how you can best position yourself in the new situation.*

◯ **Set realistic expectations:** *Understand that adapting to change might take time and there might be challenges along the way.*

◯ **Reframe the change:** *Instead of viewing change as a threat, consider looking at it as a challenge or an opportunity for growth.*

◯ **Stay curious:** *Embrace a growth mindset. Being curious can make change intriguing rather than threatening.*

◯ **Focus on what you can control:** *While certain aspects of change might be out of your control, focusing on what you can influence can empower you and reduce feelings of helplessness.*

Remember, each person's adaptability threshold and method of coping are different. It's essential to find what works best for each individual and to understand that it's okay to ask for help when needed.

And sometimes, after doing your best to navigate change and adapt as best you could, it may be the case that you simply need to leave. Like I've done in this example and many others in my career.

If you are on the receiving end of the "Bad Boss" label, and if in fact you are a poor leader or even a shitty human, you can create a different reality by navigating change with integrity *and* course correcting as necessary.

Sometimes leaders are immersed in chaos (that may be your situation right now), and this could even begin to feel normal because the organization's culture is, "Well, it's just always been that way" or "Oh, that guy, well he's just that way. Ignore him." But isn't this condition equivalent to perpetuating un-happiness or conflict in our personal lives? Why permit this?

Why not change?

Create and Practice Your Core Values:

1. Reflect on your life: *What are the experiences that have shaped you? What are the things that are most important to you? What are the things that you are passionate about? When did you feel most proud?*

2. Make a list of your core values: *After some self-reflection, identify the values that are most important to you. Make a list of up to twenty. These values may be things like honesty, integrity, compassion, respect, transparency, and joy.*

3. Define your values: *Once you have identified your values, define what each of these values means to you. How do you want to exemplify these values in your life? In other words, what do you look like, sound like, act like, and react like?*

4. Solidify your values: *Narrow your list down to those for which you would want to be known, those that most embody who and what you are as a human.*

5. Hold yourself accountable to your values by sharing them.

Here are some additional tips:

Be honest with yourself: *It can be difficult to identify and admit* *your true values. But it is important to be true to yourself so that you can live an authentic life. This is the path to Whole Human Leadership.*

Don't be afraid to change: *Your values may change over time. This is okay. As you grow and learn, your values may evolve. Permit your values to evolve as you do.*

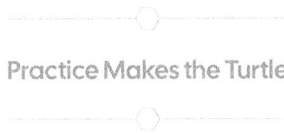

Practice Makes the Turtle

Quick Questions: Navigating Change with Authenticity

If you can answer YES to *all* of these questions, you have the authenticity of the Turtle:

○ *Do I openly communicate with my team about upcoming changes and their reasons?*

○ *Have I clearly outlined what I expect from my team in terms of managing and adapting to change?*

○ *Do I give my team autonomy and flexibility to adapt and respond to change in moments when I am not available?*

○ *Is my team invigorated when unexpected situations demand quick thinking?*

○ *Do I encourage my team to share their insights and suggestions during transitional periods?*

In periods of transition, am I able to lead and ensure the team stays aligned with our goals?

Achieving Balance at Home and at Work

When you become a Whole Human Leader, how you show up personally and professionally should mirror one another.

I used to believe that to get through life, there needed to be stability with at least one dimension of life, either personal or professional, and ideally both.

Well, I was wrong. During several pivotal years, I experienced what it was like when no part of my life felt like it was on solid footing. I experienced chronic distress that prompted me to leave a couple of companies over several years to allow me to navigate through the end of my marriage to Dee, to deal with her subsequent death from cancer, and to help my young children process their grief while trying to figure out how to process mine.

To put it simply, my work life had to complement what was happening in my personal life. I made my first professional transition to a new company around the time Dee's cancer came back after being in remission for years. That move was made without knowing the chain of horrible personal events that would follow.

The next role I took required me to travel 50 percent of the time when I started but quickly grew to upward of 75 percent. After Dee passed away, I attempted to work remotely more often, but that proved challenging in those pre-pandemic days and with my extremely client-facing role. Within six months of her death, I gave my notice. From there, I took a position with a company based in my home city of Toronto. This was the right decision for my grieving children, who needed me to be at home, not on the road, and much more available.

While I do recall shutting my office door on a few occasions to cry privately, my work performance was never negatively impacted. I held my composure at work through this very trying period of my life. Ultimately, the job change gave me the space that I needed to grieve with my children. Through it all, work provided me a place where I felt successful when so much in my home life had gone to shit.

Moving through so much change solidified what type of Whole Human Leader I wanted to be. Something in me had shifted, particularly when it came to what I value in my relationships, and in my relationship with money and material things.

I began thinking more about what success looked like, and felt like, to me.

It had nothing to do with what I owned.

I firmly decided that what I want is a life where I can make a difference that goes beyond metrics. In the divorce, I left everything but my treadmill and my clothes to Dee. I left her our home, our cottage, everything, and I started over.

"I can start all over again... again," I thought, thinking back to my childhood and how I had learned to adapt at such an early age. What I didn't understand at that point, but I certainly do now, is that I wasn't starting over. I had taken off the training wheels and was now officially riding with just two wheels on my Whole Human Leadership journey.

Skills to Develop to Navigate Change with Authenticity

Create a culture of learning for yourself:

Answer the question, "What worked about (the situation)?"

○ *Identify what you did well and what others did well.*

○ *Answer the question, "What didn't work about (the situation)?" Identify what you did wrong, what others did wrong, and, generally, what went wrong.*

○ *Answer the question, "Based on what worked and what didn't work, if I could do it all over again, what would I do differently?"*

Quick Questions: Navigating Change

○ *Can I maintain composure and concentration when facing simultaneous stresses at home and work?*

○ *Amidst life's chaos, do I prioritize my mental and physical health?*

○ *Do I have trusted individuals in both my professional and personal life to lean on during tumultuous times?*

○ *Am I able to ask for help and delegate effectively during challenging periods?*

○ *In my personal sphere, is there room for me to candidly convey my emotions?*

○ *Even in the face of overwhelming circumstances, can I decide judiciously?*

Chapter 5 Key Takeaways

Whole Human Leadership is fundamentally about staying true to your core values regardless of circumstances. Even in the face of personal tragedy, it's possible to find meaning and purpose at work.

Navigating change with authenticity leads to outcomes that are aligned with your values and with the impact you want to make at work and in your life, even when those decisions feel difficult.

Whole Human Leadership requires a high level of adaptability and resilience that can be developed by confronting challenges. When we act with authenticity, we can overcome any challenge.

Approaching change genuinely allows you to better steer the journey, resulting in a positive outcome, even if it's different from your initial expectations.

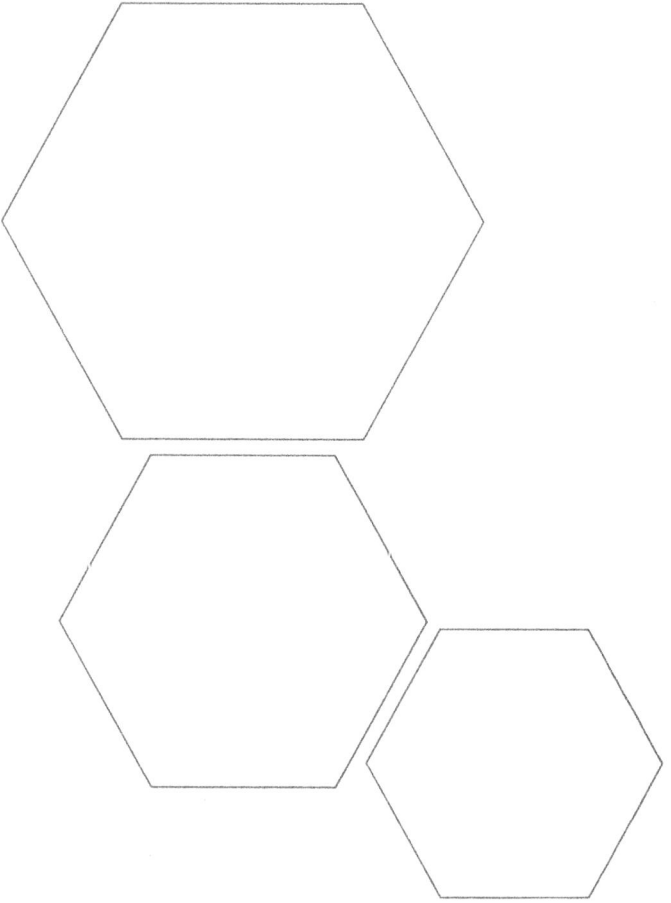

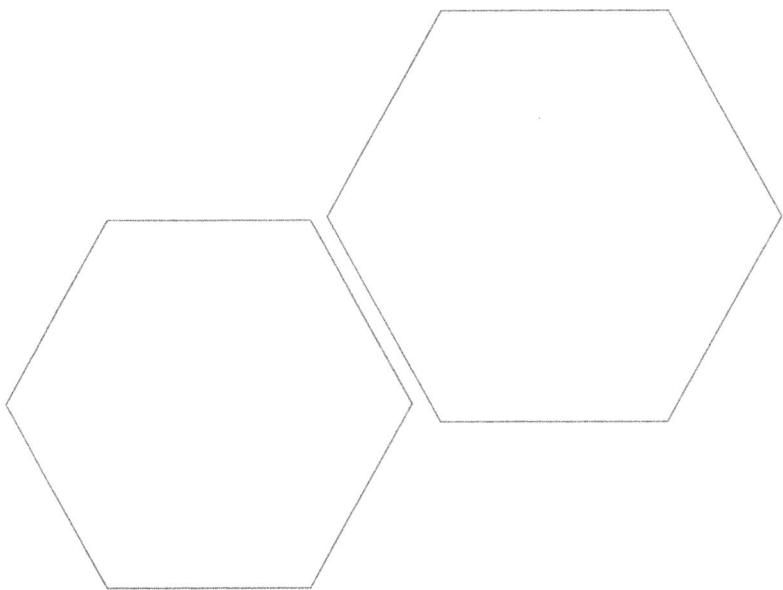

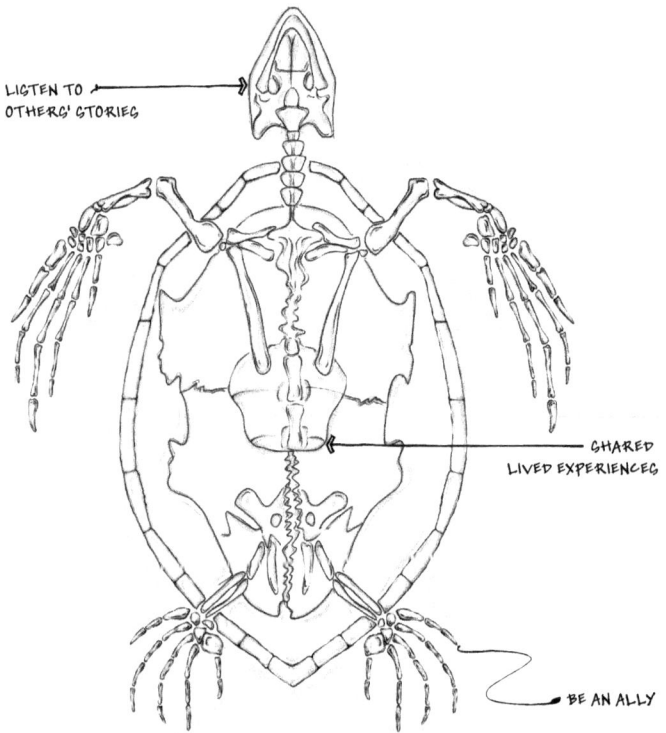

LISTEN TO
OTHERS' STORIES

SHARED
LIVED EXPERIENCES

BE AN ALLY

Chapter 6

*Advancing Diversity and Well-Being
with Empathy*

"You can't meet with this client."
Shocked, I sat listening to
Jimmy, one of our most senior
salespeople for a large organization I was
working for, tell me that he didn't want me
in an upcoming client meeting. I had been
informed that the client, like Jimmy, was
very religious, and Jimmy had made it clear
that their religion denounced same-sex relationships. As an openly queer woman—I
was married to Dee at that time—I had felt
the abrasiveness from Jimmy, but I rejected
his attempt to exclude me from a critical
client business review meeting.

At work, I strove to respect the identities
and religious beliefs of others; they did not
factor into my decision-making. I expected
the same courtesy when it came to my own
beliefs and identity. As a professional, my
focus was on fulfilling the expectations of
my role. I didn't want to dilute my time and

energy focusing on defending who I am or how I choose to live my life. It wasn't the first time that I had felt this way.

As I noted before, early in my leadership career I was almost always the youngest person at the table, and I was often the only woman.

Before I became publicly open about being a queer woman, I neutralized gender in my conversations when referencing my partner, saying things like "significant other" or "spouse." It took me time to feel comfortable being transparent. Eventually, I opened up to my closest colleagues and my direct reports that I was partnered with a woman by using accurate pronouns when referring to her. That lets people know that I am queer. Once again, I was an "only one" at the executive level, this time as the only member of the LGBTQ+ community.

I had sensed from the start of our working relationship that Jimmy was bothered by my sexuality, but it wasn't until he began trying to prevent me from doing my job that I qualified his behaviour as discrimination.

As the leader for all our client teams, my role included working with senior salespeople like Jimmy and our top clients. This particular client that Jimmy managed made up a large portion of the company's revenue. There was no way I was stepping back from interacting with any account when I felt the need to, let alone a client who was this important. Our COO, my boss, Liz, overruled Jimmy when he recommended that I shouldn't attend the meeting. She made it clear that he and I were to attend our client review meeting together, not just because we needed to show a united front amongst the company leadership, but because I was the one who was ultimately accountable for the delivery performance to this client.

In preparation for the big meeting, a colleague and I met Jimmy at his home. I'll never forget how strange it was. In the middle of our prep meeting, Jimmy took out his gun and began cleaning it while speaking to us, looking at me with disgust in his eyes nearly the entire time. When he spoke to me, he used a rude tone and continually worked to argue with nearly everything I said. I had a job to do, and I was hired to do the right thing for the client, so I stood strong without engaging his attempts to get me to react emotionally.

When his child came to say goodnight, he looked at me while speaking to him: "Don't forget to read your scriptures. God is watching." This was the most overt *and* covert, creepy expression of discrimination I have ever experienced.

There are two types of discrimination: there are little cuts of discrimination or bias that add up over time and eventually sting like hell, and then there are moments like this when you feel your personal safety is threatened.

I don't know what happened to Jimmy after the company we worked for was acquired, as we did not stay in touch. But I had no recourse with him. Because he didn't outwardly say anything about my sexuality, I let it go. Legally, the company would have needed to hear Jimmy say that he was trying to exclude me because of my sexual orientation in order to conclude that there were grounds for legal action or termination. Recognizing the challenge in front of me, I dropped the matter, as I didn't want to venture down a discouraging black hole.

Have you ever encountered an "overt/covert," Jimmy-like expression of passive-aggression at work? People may harbor any number of conscious and unconscious negative associations that produce inequality, inequity, exclusion, and sameness (think back to *The New Yorker* cartoon I discussed in Chapter 2). These can be referred to as silent, sometimes unconscious biases.[5] They say silence is golden, but in these cases, it is destructive. These overt/covert behaviours can stem from or be influenced by unfair yet persuasive, repeatedly displayed imagery and examples in our society, as well as cultural and religious beliefs.

Diversity, equity, and inclusion (DEI) are subjects that I am both passionate about and well-versed in when it comes to studies about their positive business outcomes. Convincing CEOs and executives that there are enormous opportunities to do the right thing *and* drive positive business outcomes has become easier with a large amount of research and data to back up my reasoning.[13] Because the subject of DEI could be a book of its own when it comes to becoming the Turtle, it's important to understand how empathetic exchanges of our lived experiences can help dismantle both silent bias and overt discrimination.

Let's explore this empathy aspect of DEI together in this chapter.

I'll admit, in the case of Jimmy, the eerie nature of that experience did not leave me interested in understanding his life experiences. But it did leave me knowing that I was going to continue to share mine and invite people I lead to share theirs in hopes of making a difference where I can. There are people who are open to transforming the way we relate to one another. I've found that focusing on that strength—openness—first is effective in creating more diverse and inclusive teams.

I know you are likely wanting to know what happened at the client meeting I went to with Jimmy, against his will. The meeting went incredibly well. We continued to get more work from the client. Eventually, our company was acquired, in large part due to the strength of that client relationship. While Jimmy continued to work at keeping me at arm's length from the client, I continued to be vocal to drive the effectiveness of the team so we could secure and expand the business.

Ultimately, the team that I led prevailed by maintaining an extremely high level of professionalism. The entire time I was focused on doing the right thing for the company, the team, and the client. I composted the servings of crap Jimmy kept trying to put on my plate because he didn't like me for being LGBTQ+ and used it to fertilize my drive toward positive results.

The Anatomy of Well-Being and DEI

There are over 300 species of turtles in the world. Each species has its own unique shell shape and colour. These differences are important for the species' well-being, allowing it to adapt to different environments.

Imagine a turtle's shell as your team, a compilation of thousands of lived experiences. Each bone plate in the shell represents a different employee. The plates are all different shapes and sizes, but they all work together to protect the whole.

When people from different backgrounds come together, they bring new ideas and perspectives to the table. Just as a turtle with a healthy shell is more likely to thrive, a diverse organization is more likely to perform at a higher level.[14] You cannot become the Turtle, a Whole Human Leader, with an incomplete team. Incomplete Leaders may be prone to developing incomplete teams.

Wherever you are on your leadership journey, I commend you for reading this book. Because you are on the pathway to showing up whole, committed to creating unity that drives a high-performing team, you have a huge opportunity to thrive through differences.

Your team is bonded to who you are as a Whole Leader. If you are failing at developing and leading a diverse team, I highly recommend you start doing something about it. I'm here to help you start or make further progress.

An Incomplete Leader may be unaware of their own weaknesses, or they may be unwilling to work on them. They may also be reluctant to build a diverse team, or they may not know how to do so effectively.

Are you experiencing any of these issues? Are you, maybe, fearful of the unknown? Perhaps you remain incomplete because of that fear.

If so, I propose that you overcome that fear by committing to finding a way through it. Confront your fear, and you'll find that soon enough it will likely disappear. Diversity is long overdue, and I promise you, the rewards make any discomfort you have well worth the effort.

An Incomplete Leader perpetuates sameness and inequality, whether they are conscious of it or not. The company I was working for during the Jimmy episodes is a great example of how sameness breeds groupthink and exclusion. I think it's important to share some relevant details and factual demographics about the leadership team at that company during this situation. I am providing you with these details to show you how overt/covert leadership can be formed and perpetuate a quiet and harmful ripple effect.

The CEO of the company was a white, nonreligious man whom I thought to be not only a Bad Boss but highly unprofessional and unethical. He had forced me to fire one of our employees before the employee was put onto a formal performance plan. In my opinion, that was unfair and improper. Most of the leadership team was made up of his friends and family, so it proved extremely difficult for other leaders, like my leader and COO, Liz, to challenge him. I will say that while Liz was not the Turtle, she is one of the few leaders I have respected, stuck with, and continued to stay connected to over the years. It was the leadership of the company, in my opinion, that made Liz incomplete. She did her best. Yet the Turtle does more than their best—they always stick their neck out when it comes to doing the right thing.

―――――○―――――

The Role Empathy Plays in Advancing Well-Being and DEI

―――――○―――――

A leader who remains stagnant and doesn't adapt to a global and diverse market landscape, whether by choice or oversight, poses significant risks to their stakeholders. According to the data, the absence of diversity jeopardizes innovation, efficient problem-solving, heightened employee engagement, a favourable reputation, and adherence to regulatory and legal standards.[15]

Demonstrating empathy is the master key to cultivating a holistic and diverse team. Start by making a vocal commitment. Ensure employees understand that diversity is cherished, and every individual, irrespective of their background, is embraced and esteemed. Welcome fresh perspectives and establish constructive frameworks that encourage open communication.

Innovative answers emerge from a mix of diverse viewpoints, candid feedback, and different angles.[16] Foster a team environment rooted in respect, while also emphasizing that solutions most aligned with the current mission will be the ones put into action.

Be intentional and proactively hire and elevate individuals from varied backgrounds. This goes further than just listing job vacancies on the company's site. It involves actively connecting with underrepresented communities and forging ties with entities championing diversity and inclusion. Leaders consistently striving to enrich their teams with diversity have a stronger edge in attracting and retaining the best talent.

How can we work against the overt/covert plague that has spread like wildfire in our organizations?

Diversity.

Why?

Diversity, in and of itself, is a form of accountability.

How can we convince others through our actions?

Share our lived experiences.

Why?

Empathy breeds compassion and understanding.

Understanding is wise.

Wisdom listens intently and acts on behalf of well-trained intuition.

The Turtle modernizes the landscape of work through the diversity of the workforce. There's been significant evolution. In honour of the Long Game of Leadership, you better start training for the marathon. Or at least catch-up and keep pace. Empathy is the key.

Skills to Develop Empathy

Listen to the stories of people from different backgrounds. *This can be done through personal conversations, reading books and articles, or watching documentaries.*

Be open to learning about different cultures and perspectives. *This can be done by travelling, taking classes, or joining clubs or organizations that promote diversity and inclusion.*

Be supportive of marginalized groups. *This can be done by speaking out against discrimination, donating to charities that support marginalized groups, or volunteering your time to help marginalized groups.*

Share your own lived experiences with others. *This can help others to understand your perspective and to learn from your experiences.*

---◇---

Practice Makes the Turtle

---◇---

Quick Questions: Advancing Diversity and Well-Being with Empathy

If you can answer YES to *all* of these questions, you have the empathy of the Turtle:

Based on unbiased feedback, such as anonymous staff surveys, do you believe you're perceived positively as a leader?

Do you view diversity not only as a moral imperative but also as beneficial for business?

When considering diversity, do you recognize its vast scope and consider intersectionality (which is the recognition of the complex interplay of diverse identities)? This includes age, race, sexual orientation, disability, and beyond.

Can you confidently claim that you demonstrate how you value and respect your employees, and empower them to give their best?

Are you committed to a data-driven approach in DEI to identify gaps, establish goals, and measure growth more effectively?

Are you an advocate for diversity and inclusion initiatives, and do you maintain a method for self-accountability?

Do you offer a platform through employee resource groups (ERGs) for your staff to interact, relay personal experiences, and foster change within the enterprise?

Chapter 6 Key Takeaways

Empathy is essential for creating a diverse and inclusive workplace. Create a culture where everyone feels valued and respected. This includes having policies and procedures in place to prevent discrimination and harassment.

Diversity, equity, and inclusion drive positive business outcomes. Make DEI a priority. Set goals for DEI and track your progress over time.

Promote diversity and inclusion in your hiring practices. Make sure to recruit candidates from diverse backgrounds.

Be an ally. Speak up when you see discrimination or harassment occurring. We can all play a role in promoting diversity, equity, and inclusion by listening to the stories of people, especially those different from ourselves.

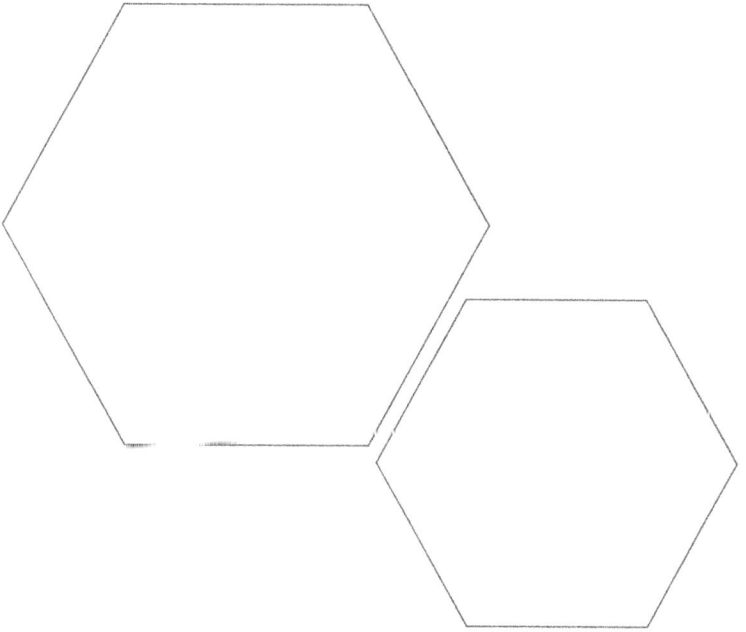

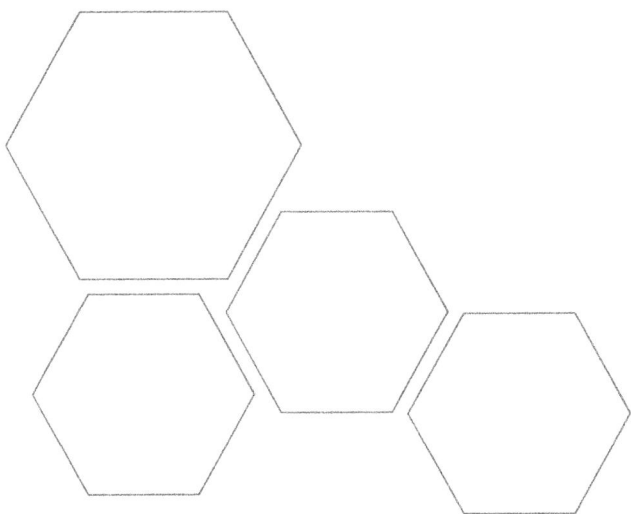

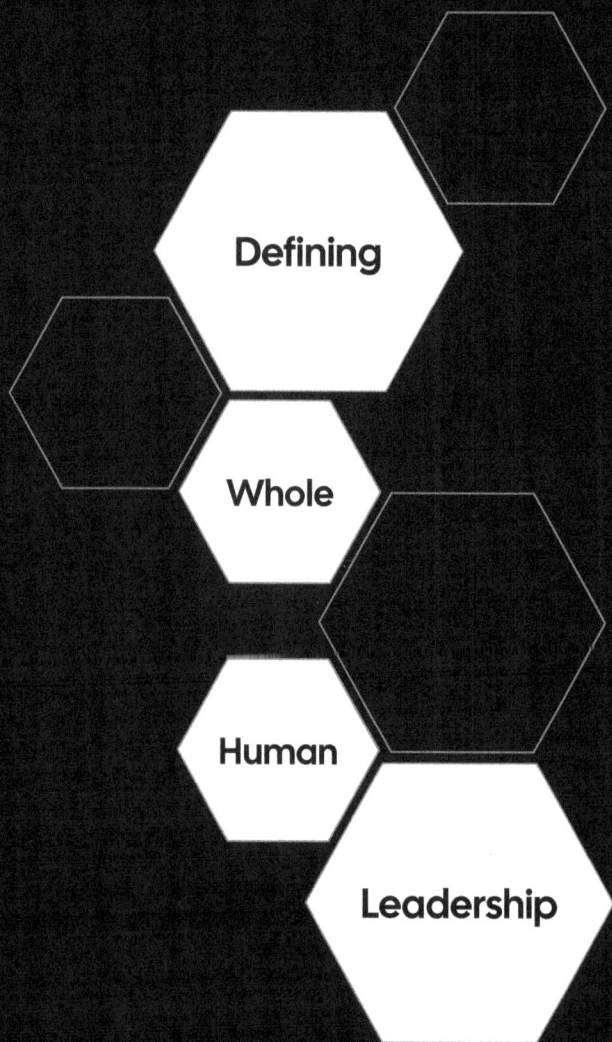

Defining

Whole

Human

Leadership

> *"Authenticity is a collection of choices that we have to make every day.*
> *It's about the choice to show up and be real.*
> *The choice to be honest.*
> *The choice to let our true selves be seen."*

— **Brené Brown**
The Gifts of Imperfection

Part 4

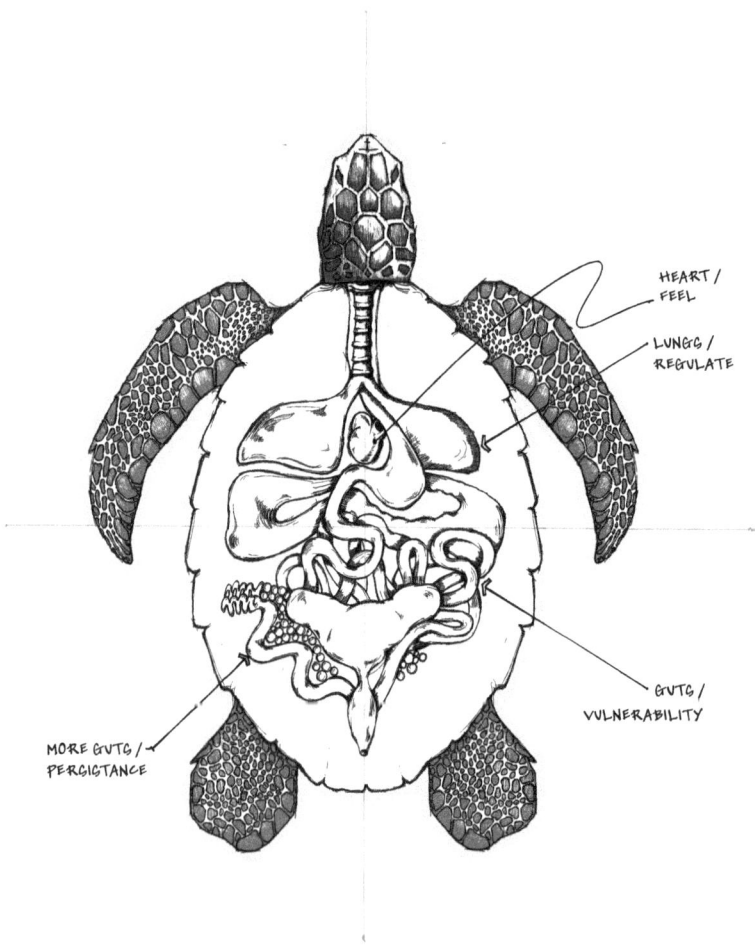

HEART /
FEEL

LUNGS /
REGULATE

GUTS /
VULNERABILITY

MORE GUTS /
PERSISTANCE

Chapter 7

Successful Failure and Humble Success

Racial discrimination? I was being named *personally* in an employee's legal threat for terminating him, and he claimed the reason was racial discrimination? This was supposed to happen to leaders who were not focused on diversity, those who hired people who looked like them. The kind of leader who sifts through resumes, bypassing those with more ethnic-sounding names or geographically diverse college or work experience. Being named in such lawsuits is something that should happen to leaders who *are* racist. Or Jimmy, the guy who had no reason for discriminating against me except for the fact that his religion condemns a woman marrying a woman, as I had.

I did not imagine a queer woman with an impeccable history in creating diverse teams would be named personally in a wrongful termination suit, certainly not one where the accuser claimed to have been terminated because of the colour of his skin.

Five of the last seven people I had last hired were people of colour, and one of them was Mike, the employee who named me in his legal action.

At 27 years old, I was still showing up as the Iron Maiden, but I certainly wasn't, nor ever have been, racist. I was an Incomplete Leader in terms of bringing my whole self to work, but I *always* brought advocacy, intentionality, and action in my work around diversity, equity, and inclusion. Always.

The company was the primary target of the legal action. Knowing that I had done an effective job managing Mike and subsequently exiting him within his probationary period, I started gathering supporting evidence for the termination to fight his claim.

Through the interview process, before he accepted the job, I presented the role and expectations of the position to him in detail. Every question he asked was answered. Expectations, success metrics, and outcomes were set with transparency. After he was hired, I held weekly one-on-one meetings with him so I could ensure that he was adjusting well. I let him know that I was there to help him overcome any barriers to being success-ful. Shortly after he started, it was clear that Mike was struggling in his role, which was to manage an underperforming team and begin performance management processes with many of its members.

Within six weeks of his starting, I sat him down and began to coach him and provide tools and resources to help him improve. Providing real-time feedback has always been important to me. Surprising employees by stalling critical, performance-related feedback was never my style. I considered leaders like that to be cowards.

Despite my coaching, it became clear that I had to put Mike on a performance plan. It was the best pathway, providing no room for misunderstandings, particularly during his three-month probation period. Once the performance plan was in place, I knew from experience that he would either remain employed or manage himself out. My goal was *always* retention. I was the Turnaround Queen and, yes, that meant that I had to do this hundreds of times, managing individual performance and terminating those unable to successfully deliver. Increased retention and engagement were my top priorities, but terminations were inevitable. Ultimately, I was confident in making hard decisions on behalf of our stakeholders.

Our human resource and legal teams decided to pay Mike out to prevent a costly lawsuit. This was hard for me to accept as it felt like a tacit acknowledgement of his claim, but I understood the cost analysis for the decision. I hated that they settled, but I understood the rationale.

Yet, I still felt like I failed the company. Accused of something I didn't do and being someone or something that I wasn't, I had officially lived out one of my worst leadership nightmares. Although not a long and drawn-out legal battle, it haunted me. I did a lot of reflecting and reviewing of the situation, from my first interview with Mike to the day he was terminated. I knew I had been effective in my leadership, my coaching, and, ultimately, my decision to terminate him, but the situation still felt like a failure.

Looking back on hiring Mike twenty years ago, I now regret I didn't delve deeper into his leadership experience during the interviewing process. Before hiring him, I had shared with Mike how the team he was going to lead required significant performance management. I let him know that he would need to have some very difficult conversations with team members, the types of conversations that even the most seasoned leaders often struggle with. If I had asked questions that better probed his past experience in this regard and his comfort level with what was being asked of him, perhaps I would have been able to foresee that he was not the right hire. Seeing his leadership skills, it became clear almost immediately that there were significant shortcomings.

Do you recall the situation in Chapter 3 about how I tried to win over Kate, the tough New Yorker, and the pivotal moment when I spoke up and claimed responsibility for her team and its delivery issue? Well, the situation with Mike also required me to take responsibility, this time for my own error in hiring. In the end, this was my failure, and I took accountability for it.

What I took away from both situations was that I could find success in failure by identifying what I did well, what I could have done better, and what I learned from the experience. But the "successful failure" doesn't stop there. As I went through the process of finding Mike's replacement, I invested much more time and asked very different questions to ensure that I was making the right hire.

The Anatomy of Successfully Failing as the Turtle

When you are dealing with failure, you have a golden opportunity to turn a bad situation into a positive one, or at least a not-so-bad one that doesn't leave you full of regret. But to do this, you need to marshall all of the skills and resources of your whole human, whole turtle self.

I use a four-step approach to fail successfully:

1. I recognize that there is always some good in the bad. I ac-

knowledge the areas where I *was* successful or did excel during this challenging period.

2. I reflect on my errors and areas of potential improvement. This requires deep, sometimes difficult, thinking, so I take my time with it.

3. I derive insights and best practices to carry into future endeavours.

4. I implement what I've learned to prevent reoccurrence.

In Mike's case, it was clear I had to think critically and objectively about my hiring process. I clearly didn't dig deep enough with Mike.

As I went through this analysis process, the question I had been asking myself —"What was he *thinking*?"—turned into "What had he experienced in his life to drive him to do something so unfair?" While I never got the answer from him, I didn't need it to imagine different scenarios that may have contributed to him falsely accusing me of wrongdoing. Honestly, I wasn't trying to give him a fair break for it. I had to ask questions that would help me make sense of something so senseless.

After everything settled down, I was even more committed to creating a diverse workplace. I knew that this was an opportunity to provide more opportunities for people who were also driven to do the right thing.

Skills for Successfully Failing

Develop healthy mechanisms for coping with the stress caused by failure. *Turn to exercise, meditation, or spending time with loved ones, and mark these successes, both big and small, as a reminder of your capabilities.*

Find solitude. *In the midst of failure, it's easy to become over-whelmed. Taking time out to be alone and find quiet can give you time to self-reflect.*

Challenge yourself to find your responsibility in every situation. *We always play a part in failure. Stand up and verbalize the part that you feel responsible for.*

Read books or study people in history who have failed. *Failure is a natural part of growth. Learning from successful people who have shared their feelings about failure can be an inspiring practice; it can help you see the opportunities that emerge when things don't work out the way you planned.*

Skills for Humble Success

Offer positive feedback. Cultivate a culture where your team regularly receives and extends praise and encouragement, especially during group discussions.

Draw insights from your team. Celebrate victories with your team and openly acknowledge the lessons they've imparted to you. Make sure they're aware of their positive influence.

Acknowledge genuine accomplishments. Regularly highlight both collective and individual achievements in group and one-on-one settings.

Mentor your team in the art of humble victories. Post-accomplishment, convene to discuss strategies that were effective, areas for improvement, and adaptations for future endeavours.

————————◯————————

Practice Makes the Turtle

————————◯————————

Quick Questions: Successfully Failing and Succeeding with Humility

If you can answer YES to *all* of these questions, you have the ability to learn, grow and adapt as the ways of the Turtle:

○ *Can I openly acknowledge when I'm accountable for failure?*

○ *Do I consistently use insights gleaned from past mistakes to foster my growth?*

○ *Have I cultivated methods, such as meditation or physical activity, to manage the emotional aftermath of setbacks or failure?*

○ *In moments of significant accomplishments, do I use "we" to emphasize collective achievement?*

○ *Do I set aside moments to appreciate the team's achievements and acknowledge individual efforts?*

○ *Am I proactive in supporting and promoting promising team members, even if it might result in their departure from my group?*

Uplifting Others So They Can Shine and Succeed

In the twenty years after Mike initiated his legal action, I have graced hundreds of stages speaking about DEI and Whole Human Leadership. During that time, I have acquired another nickname, the CEO Whisperer, for my ability to stimulate change from the top by convincing CEOs of structural and behavioural changes that needed to be made to improve the quality of the leadership and workplace culture in their companies. My most satisfying business accomplishments over the years have been those where I have helped other people succeed.

One that I'm most proud of was when I had been relocated back to the US and was leading a large Americas business unit. We held a large, in-person gathering where I was able to meet much of my new team face-to-face. It was here that I met Roger. You know how you meet someone, and you just immediately *know* they are a great human being? That was how I felt when I met Roger. I remember thinking to myself upon meeting him, "Oh, this is going to be *good*!"

Within a few months of being in my position, it was time for our annual performance review cycle. I had received emails from all of Roger's direct reports. He led an all-female team, and they took it upon themselves to spell out what a wonderful leader he was and how he had helped advance their careers.

Astoundingly, Roger had only been at the company for a couple of years. He was one level below our executive level. In a one-on-one meeting, he shared with me that he wanted to become an executive, to make partner someday.

It wasn't only Roger's high-performing team singing his praises. His clients loved him too. That said, Roger hadn't achieved all the financial and business metrics typically required by our company to be promoted to partner, especially given certain worldwide and economic headwinds that had impacted the business as a whole.

But then a very significant racially motivated attack occurred, rocking much of the US. Roger was very open to sharing his lived experience as an African-American man in the US, but in the wake of this event, he stepped up within our organization to create a greater understanding of his personal experience, and he even helped reverse-mentor one of the senior leaders in the company. It's a rarity to find a changemaker like Roger.

So began the heart of my work with Roger. I was determined to see him excel and become a partner at our company. I made it my mission to ensure that he had a platform for success and was in front of many of the key decision-makers in the company. This included having him invited to the company's leadership training programs, getting him engaged in high-profile projects, and advocating for him at every opportunity possible.

When I resigned from our company, Roger was a final candidate to be promoted to partner. My leaving was difficult for both of us as I had so wanted to be there to see him succeed and he was aware that I was one of his biggest supporters and sponsors. To ensure my advocacy for his promotion was included in the process, I recorded a video that he would be able to use for the selection committee.

When he later called me to tell me the wonderful news that he had made it, I remember thinking how incredible it was to have been able to provide resources, support, and a framework for someone else to realize their dream. In the end, I feel that it was my privilege to have been his advocate and sponsor for the time we worked together.

The Anatomy of Humble Success as the Turtle

Humble success is a Whole Human, Whole Turtle act. I employ a four-phase approach to achieve success with humility:

1. I recognize the elements that contributed to achieving a positive outcome.

2. I attribute the success to the involved individuals or teams.

3. I determine additional steps I can take to further amplify future achievements.

4. I implement insights gained to replicate similar successes.

Humble success originates from a genuine place, beginning with the awareness about who is in the room. Without the platform I endeavoured to create, would Roger have remained the Unseen Employee? I believe not. He earned, in his own right, the executive role that he was promoted to, but I had the privilege of being one of those who facilitated opportunities for him. Our bond was immediate, rooted in mutual trust. He confided in me because I genuinely sought to grasp his narrative and understand his mission.

In vast corporate landscapes, ascending the ranks necessitates senior leaders advocating for and championing standout team members. Without such advocacy, talented, ambitious, and high-potential performers may remain in the shadows due to the sheer scale of the organization. If they do, there's a heightened chance they will seek opportunities elsewhere.

Achieving with humility means stepping back and letting others shine in the spotlight. It's an understanding that, as a leader, your primary role is to cultivate an environment where individuals flourish. By investing time in understanding each team member, facilitating one-on-one weekly discussions, educating, mentoring, and unlocking opportunities for the deserving, you embody the essence of the Turtle. Your focus isn't on retaining every individual out of fear of their advancement. Instead, your vision is to foster a multitude of Turtles, empowering them to ascend to influential positions and reshaping the landscape for a brighter future.

Chapter 7 Key Takeaways

Doing significant due diligence through the recruitment process is a worthwhile effort that will save you significant time, money, and energy in the long run.

A Whole Human Leader takes responsibility for mistakes. Even when you've done everything correctly, if issues arise, acknowledge them and use them as learning opportunities.

Embrace the possibility of failure. Everyone encounters setbacks; the key is to glean lessons from them and make informed moves going forward.

A Whole Human Leader uplifts others. Serve as a mentor, sponsor, or champion for those pursuing their goals.

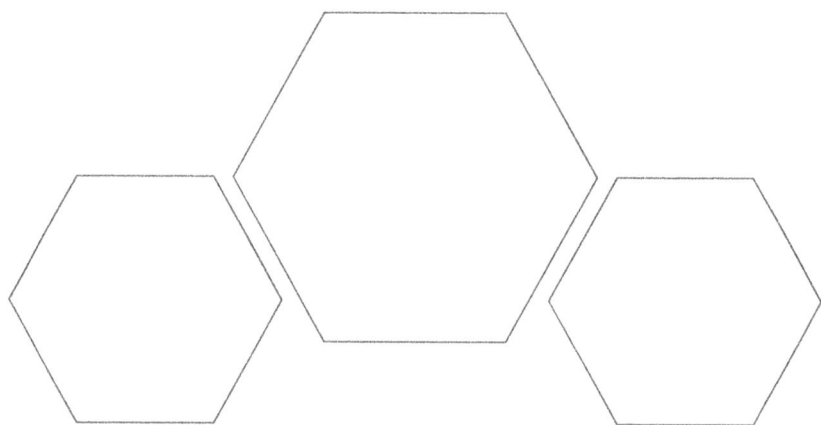

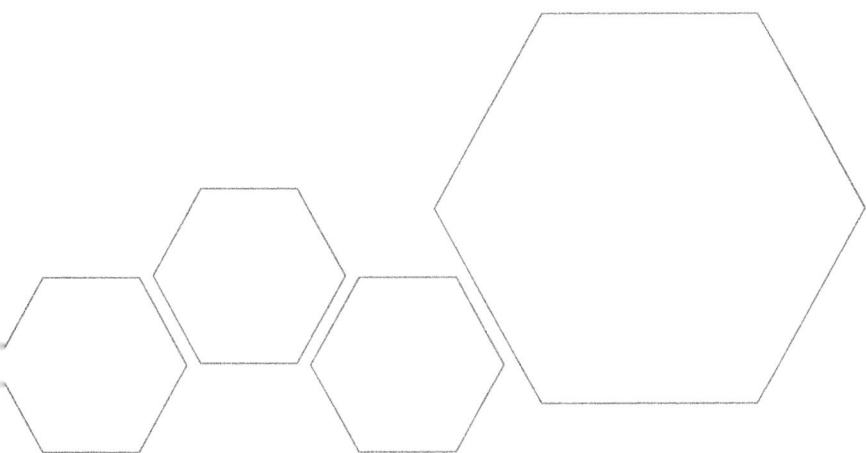

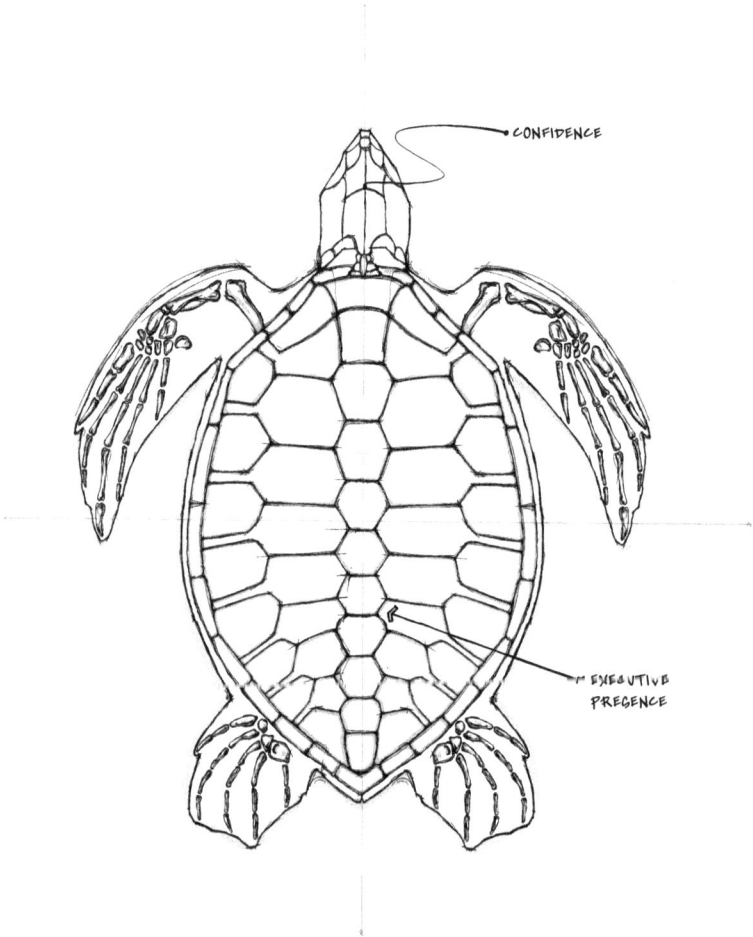

CONFIDENCE

EXECUTIVE PRESENCE

Chapter 8

*Developing Your Whole Human
Personalized Leadership Style*

Mary was incredible with clients. Every time she walked into a meeting, she graced the room with positive energy and a solutions-based mindset. Having come from a lower socio-economic background, she did not have a college degree. What she did have was what is so often referred to in leadership parlance as "the things you can't teach." Her innate drive and determination, coupled with her being extremely coachable, made Mary stand out from colleagues with higher levels of formal education. Her lived experience had likely influenced her strengths, but it had also negatively affected her ability to show up, exuding the level of professionalism needed to help her grow into a leadership position.

The big issue was Mary's insecurity about her not having a college degree. Rather than leading with her impressive and very pertinent skills and talents, she would instead regularly make mention of her lack of formal education, bringing pointless attention to her Achilles heel.

Unfortunately, early in Mary's career with us, a member of the senior leadership team had mentioned to her that her lack of education meant that her growth would be inhibited. It seemed like she was forever carrying that feedback with her in a heavy "backpack." I made it my goal to help her unpack this useless burden so she could advance.

However, there was one additional factor that was holding Mary back from being seen as a leader. Rather than wearing more professional business attire, she showed up at work often looking like she was going to a nightclub. While I stand by the value of personal expression, I also believe that the way we show up physically, and our executive presence at work is a part of what defines us as leaders.

For several years in our one-on-one meetings, I coached Mary on her professional presence, helping her find her own unique style. That wasn't all, though. I also worked with her on becoming a more whole human at work, taking down the barriers to her growth through the model of the Turtle anatomy.

Executive Presence Versus Whole Human Leadership

I first learned of the term "Executive Presence" from other executives who sat at the table with me. The term was originated by author Sylvia Anne Hewlett and is defined in her book, *Executive Presence: The Missing Link Between Merit and Success*, as the way one acts (gravitas), speaks (communication), and looks (appearance).[17] I've often used the term because I appreciate the definition, as set forth by Hewlett. However, as I explain below,

I have found it necessary when I address the issue of Executive Presence to integrate the Whole Human Leadership anatomy into the conversation. Doing so supports the person I am coaching in creating a more authentic Executive Presence based on key behaviour traits and learned skills of the Turtle.

I believe that an individual's Executive Presence will remain incomplete or inappropriately developed in the absence of the Turtle anatomy. In fact, I believe that in the very process of becoming the Turtle, there's a natural actualization of Executive Presence. Another issue I have found with Executive Presence is that it can easily be interpreted or utilized to exclude women. Given that large corporations still lack equity in female leadership representation, today's leadership style is based on the past leadership style, which was primarily made up of men.

In an article from *Forbes* in 2021, it is noted that S&P Global came out with an analysis by researchers from the University of Paris with findings that female CEOs "illustrated greater empathy, adaptability, and diversity more frequently than their male peers, per a survey of 8,500 companies across 61 countries. Words like empathy, intuition, compromise, and compassion have been viewed as soft in previous decades but now are viewed as increasingly necessary in the workplace—perhaps even a strategic imperative."[18]

Plain and simple, the legacy version of Executive Presence, which does not incorporate the elements of the Turtle, has been historically based on male leadership styles, or rather gender stereotypes of leadership and behavioural traits. Going forward, the growing diversity in leadership teams will help establish a Whole Human Leadership version of Executive Presence, thereby reducing the potential discrimination against or exclusion of women and unseen employees. There is value in Executive Presence, but like most practices that exist in the workforce today, inclusivity will give it a modern upgrade.

As mentioned, *Executive Presence: The Missing Link Between Merit and Success* posits three main elements of a successful Executive Presence:

1. Gravitas (how you act)
2. Communication (how you speak)
3. Appearance (how you look)

The idea is that you can work on these components of success to build an image that attracts a bigger followership. This is absolutely correct, and I am in no way arguing with any of this. You *can* attract followers this way.

However, while there's a slight undertone of Whole Human Leadership present in the term, I have observed a disconnect in how Executive Presence has been translated into action by leaders. When implemented ineffectively, Executive Presence can be interpreted as excluding people who don't match the pattern matching that has been based on the predominantly stereotypical male leadership style or traits that was referenced in Chapter 2: "The Unseen Employee: Completing Your Team." I believe that the concept—at least how I've seen it adopted by some leaders and organizations—perpetuates the algorithm that prevents diversity and originality in the workplace.

It's important to note that I am not against the leadership and behavioural traits that are typically characterized as more masculine; in fact, I possess many of them myself. That is why I believe diversity is not just a moral imperative but is justified by having been proven to drive business results. There are a vast amount of data points to support positive outcomes related to more diverse leadership teams, including advanced innovation, boosting productivity, and increasing engagement.

As I've emphasized, I firmly hold that diversity is not only a moral obligation but also a catalyst for superior business results. The extent to which you can embody your unique version of the Turtle is directly linked to the diversity of your team and their ability to operate at peak performance.

At its core, Executive Presence (from its original perspective) is adopted as a remedy to improve external appearance, confidence, and behaviour. I have found it best to be cautious with whom I use this phrase. Why? Because I believe, based on what I have witnessed and experienced firsthand, that an unnuanced focus on Executive Presence has the potential to breed Iron Maiden-like leadership qualities in certain people.

There's a torturous element to Executive Presence. The iron-maiden-like spikes poke holes in a leader who is more focused on appearance than embodying true leadership. To me, the term lacks a certain genuine, humanizing sentiment. Ultimately, if your actions, words, and appearance are driven by a desire for status or to prove a point, you will remain incomplete and unfulfilled.

Executive Presence is incomplete without Whole Human Leadership. It's like saying "Be yourself," but here, let me give you a guide to tell you how to act, speak, and look. In Whole Human Leadership, the guide for how you show up is an internal driver. This guide will direct your actions based on what motivates you to make a positive impact through the great power and responsibility you have as a leader.

If you focus on Executive Presence in the absence of emotional intelligence and empathy, you will lack authenticity. If your focus is on getting followers rather than creating more Whole Human Leaders, you and your team will be incomplete. Yes, you want to be a leader who people want to follow, but there's a difference between creating blind followers and self-led followers.

Again, I don't think that Executive Presence is wrong. However, I do think that its precepts may result in something that does not support Whole Human Leadership and may keep you and your team in a place of "faking it until you make it."

Operating every single day through misalignment of your

purpose and core values is inevitable if you ignore doing the necessary work that begins within you.

Let's look at a side-by-side examination of "legacy" Executive Presence and Whole Human Leadership:

Legacy Executive Presence (Outside)	Whole Human Leadership (Inside Out)
Prove Something	*Create Something*
A Monologue Keen Senses	*A Movement*
Gravitas (How You Act)	*Authenticity* (Where You Act From)
Communication (How You Speak)	*Tone* (Where You Speak From)
Appearance (How You Look)	*Confidence* (The Energy You Exude)
Perpetuates Old Leadership Ideas	*Exemplifies Modern Leadership Essentials*

You may disagree with my assertion that Executive Presence is incomplete without the qualities added by Whole Human Leadership. Perhaps the legacy version of Executive Presence *has* worked for you so far and maybe gotten you a seat at the table like it did me. But would you be reading this book if it was still working?

How Whole Human Leadership Advances Your Career

Whole Human Leadership takes you to the next level. When you come forth whole, you won't have to learn how to act, how to speak, or how to modify your appearance for success. All of that will come naturally and effortlessly when you permit the original, authentic, values-based *you* to present itself.

Recently, Mary contacted me asking me to be an employment reference. I was thrilled to hear that in the years since we last worked together, she had advanced professionally and overcome the barriers that once prevented her from reaching her goals. It had taken her time and practice, but she kept pace and, as a result, is now happy and thriving as she evolves into a Whole Human Leader.

Whole Human Leadership is, at its core, about *attraction*, while Executive Presence focuses on making sure you do not create *dis*tractions in how you present yourself. Through conditioning and strengthening yourself first, you will develop a powerful ability to lead your team to perform at the highest level. Together, you can start playing the Long Game of Leadership as Mary has instead of running a series of sprints that leave you too exhausted to enjoy your success.

I have shared the stories in this book with the goal of inspiring you to create your distinct, personalized style of Whole Human Leadership. You have now been fully introduced to the conceptual anatomy of the Whole Human Leader and have been given key points of comprehension, along with skills to develop and practice.

Now what?

It's time for you to define and create your *own* version of the Turtle. No two leaders are alike (and that's a good thing!). Now you get to learn how to lead as a Whole Human Leader *your* way!

In the rest of this chapter, I'm going to ask you to engage in various exercises that will help you design your own personal style of leadership. But first, let's establish a few ground rules before we get started:

1. Be radically honest with yourself going forward. Admit to yourself where you are experiencing rough patches between leaving the Incomplete Leader behind and evolving into the Whole Human Leader. Always hold yourself accountable, but don't judge yourself too sternly. This is a challenging process. Also—especially during this early phase—I don't recommend that you necessarily share your leadership transformation effort with others. Keep it to yourself for a while until you're on firmer footing.

2. Do not blame yourself for where you are in your journey. Remember, we are all fallible and make mistakes. Allow yourself grace as you transform, and make space for the leader you are becoming.

3. Avoid justifying your past actions or behaviours. Recognize that leadership can often be isolating, and it might seem daunting not to revert to previous "comfortable" leadership styles. Initially, resisting the urge to conform can be challenging, but over time your evolved leadership style will come to feel innate. You're not in the wrong. You just haven't been shown how to be your own version of the Turtle.

Dan Sullivan, the well-known founder of Strategic Coach, wrote the book *Who Not How*, which has become hugely popular with successful executives and entrepreneurs.[19] The strength of this book lies in its simple advice of focusing on who can assist you in achieving your desired outcomes instead of how to achieve them. Essentially, dwelling on how can clutter our minds, pushing us to solve everything independently instead of effectively delegating to those more skilled at certain tasks. However, using the strengths of other people allows us to truly lead without getting bogged down in the details.

What about when "who" is *you*?

In Whole Human Leadership, you are *who* when it comes to confronting challenges head-on, creating a purpose-driven team, holding yourself and the team accountable, and doing what's right based on your core values and what's good for the people you lead. This is the role you accepted and the commitment you made to the company. You are *who* is stepping up by filling in the gaps that stand between you and Whole Human Leadership so that you can connect with the people on your team, the people who are essential to the success of the business.

Can you tell me exactly what it is I need to do to be a Whole Human Leader (aka the Turtle)?

Yes, I can.

First, allow me to briefly go back in time with you to when I would watch the television shows *LA Law* and *Dallas* with my mom. It turns out that I didn't become a lawyer, and while I might carry some attributes of Patricia Ewing, Victoria Principal's character in *Dallas*, I would say that's where the resemblance ends. I realized that I didn't have anyone to look up to in my life. Maybe you're fortunate to have a Turtle in your life. If so, that is extremely valuable.

Suppose you, much like me, are driven to excel beyond the confines of your life's circumstances, aspiring for a grander vision of your existence, and have adopted the Turtle-like qualities described in this book. In that case, you are well on your way to shaping your version of Whole Human Leadership. Remember: each turtle, akin to humans, is unique in its own way.

The Turtle journey reflects the vision I have had for myself, starting when I was a teenager, of a young woman who knew that she could be so much bigger and better than her abused and rejected start to life might indicate. Coming forth as the Iron Maiden did yield initial outward career success, yes, but when I released myself from *all business, all of the time*, I started playing the Long Game of Leadership. Being an Incomplete Leader would not have been sustainable for me. More than likely, I would have reached a plateau in my level of success or, even worse, been unfulfilled and unsatisfied in my work. The difficult personal development I went through in learning how to bring my whole self to work helped me understand how capable I can be in *all* areas of my life.

It's your turn to create your personalized Whole Human Leadership style.

Your Private Workshop: Defining Your Personal Leadership Style

For now, I ask you to place *everything* aside except for yourself and something to write with (a digital tool or a physical notepad; you decide).

I began as the Iron Maiden.

Where are you beginning?

Let's start with the *before* to your *after* by confronting your hardest truths. How incomplete do you consider yourself to be as a leader? This is not an exercise in shame but rather a preliminary look in the mirror that will allow you to release what's been getting in your way.

Given that you are reading this book, even this far along, I'm betting that there is currently a level of incompleteness you are experiencing as a leader. This far into the reading, it's also probable that you're beginning to *change* your behaviour. More than likely, you have uncovered certain insights into how you show up at work that will prove to be useful as you build your personalized Whole Human Leadership style. Or on the contrary, perhaps you haven't initiated any changes yet. No matter how complete or incomplete you think you are right now, I assure you you are on the right path and I encourage you to stay the course.

Knowing what's not working is the base for effective problem-solving. The not-so-good-looking truth is the foundation by which you can measure your progress going forward. Rest assured, after this, we will examine your strengths, which is the ultimate focus of Whole Human Leadership. It may feel challenging to start by confronting your truths. But by doing so, you will go beyond your past and into a zone where your strengths will become more apparent.

I invite you to use this list to identify behaviours you might be currently displaying that are associated with the Incomplete Leader (aka, for me, the Iron Maiden). Review this list and make note of any of the descriptions that represent how you are currently showing up, even if only a small percentage of the time.

The Profile of the Incomplete Leader

You perceive leadership as a strict hierarchy:

○ *You might harbour thoughts like "I'm the boss" or even voice them.*

○ *You expect your team to seek approval for tasks beyond their designated roles to keep tabs on their progress.*

You're unaware of the personal motivations and purpose of your team members:

◯ *Initial moments in one-on-one meetings don't focus on building rapport or connection.*

◯ *The deeper motivations of the team members reporting to you remain a mystery.*

When failures occur, your first instinct is to pinpoint who's to blame:

◯ *You find it challenging to accept that you bear the weight of the team's successes and failures, but the accolades shouldn't be solely yours.*

◯ *When faced with an underperforming team member, you hesitate instead of promptly addressing the issue.*

When you enter your workplace, be it physically or virtually, you adopt a distinct persona, different from your at-home self:

◯ *You feel uncomfortable or may believe it to be inappropriate to show emotion with the team.*

◯ *The stress from your personal life, which you might be concealing, adversely affects you, leading to negative feelings and responses at work. This can also spill over into your home life, where you inadvertently vent your work frustrations. This burden is becoming too heavy for you to bear.*

Now that you have reviewed the list let's segue to moving another step closer to creating your personalized Whole Human Leadership style.

Ask yourself, "Am I taking action on behalf of Whole Human Leadership?" Before you act or respond when stimuli arise, ask this simple question to help you decipher whether you are acting on behalf of the Turtle.

Then, repeat the question to prompt the next response and action, and the next. With every choice comes an opportunity to recalibrate and align what you do and say with what you want.

Over time, by consistently directing yourself toward Whole Human Leadership, the more natural and automatic it will become to operate with the behaviour traits of the Turtle. You will know when you are Incomplete. It will become more and more obvious to you when you are out of alignment and, therefore, easier to correct. When you reach the point of no longer having to ask yourself whether you are Incomplete or Whole (but I do recommend doing this from time to time anyway), you will have likely arrived at Whole Human Leadership.

Prepare your notebook.
Read the following prompts and begin writing.

Using the thoughts you had and the notes you took as you went through the list of behavioural traits of the Incomplete Leader, answer the following questions:

◇ *What are some words you would use to describe yourself as an Incomplete Leader?*

◇ *If you were to give yourself a nickname as an Incomplete Leader, what would it be? If you have already been given one, like I had (the Iron Maiden), what is it?*

○ *Is there a degree of truth in the nickname in terms of your behaviour?*

○ *What is untrue about the moniker in terms of who you know yourself to be?*

○ *What valuable parts of you are you keeping hidden away in the heavy backpack during work hours?*

○ *How is that affecting your leadership style?*

Now, let's move from Incomplete to Whole, shall we?

Regardless of how you describe your unique Whole Leadership Style, visualizing a Turtle's anatomy can guide you in identifying your current strengths and weaknesses. Imagine each segment of the shell as a space you can fill with colour, but to do so, you must excel in that area.

For instance, during my Iron Maiden phase, I was proficient in critical thinking, advancing diversity, and navigating change. However, I wasn't as adept in emotional intelligence, authenticity, or empathy. It's not that I lacked these traits entirely, I just didn't prominently display them in professional settings. Take authenticity, for instance. While I did uphold my core personal values and made tough decisions aligned with them, I wasn't wholly genuine at work. Thus, I would leave that segment unfilled.

Next, identify the parts that you are not able to colour in. Suppose you have more than one part of the shell that cannot be filled in. In that case, I recommend that you approach the development of the behaviour traits of the Turtle in the order listed below rather than at random because developing from the top down will help you more fluently develop into a Whole Human Leader. To further gauge your progress, you can revisit the Practice Makes the Turtle questions:

○ *Critical Thinking and Emotional Intelligence (chapter 3, page 71)*

○ *Empathy and Authenticity (chapter 4, page 86)*

○ *Ability to Navigate Change (chapter 5, page 105)*

○ *Commitment to Diversity (chapter 6, page 123)*

○ *Succeeding with Humility (chapter 7, page 139)*

○ *Failing Successfully (chapter 7, page 139)*

I became the Turtle. Who are you becoming?

It's time to start working on who *you* want to be.

The Whole Human Leader (aka the Turtle).

There's a good chance you already embody this persona in certain facets of your life or around specific individuals. Yet, by reaching this point in the book, you probably recognize how much more efficient, influential, and fulfilled you'd be if more people in the workplace experienced this side of you. Imagine the ways your evolved leadership style can boost team engagement and performance.

I invite you to use this list to identify behaviours you might be currently displaying that are associated with Whole Human Leadership.

The Whole Human Leader:

○ *Your leadership approach is rooted in collaboration and support, giving equal importance to every team member's strengths and contributions.*

○ *You champion a culture marked by trust, transparency, and empowerment. You entrust your team with decision-making, recognizing their competencies and capabilities.*

○ *You invest in understanding the unique ambitions and objectives of each team member. Through one-on-one sessions, you focus on forging relationships, building rapport, and aiding them in realizing their personal dreams.*

○ *You recognize the significance of each team member's individual purpose and well-being. You strive to align their personal objectives with their roles, offering consistent support.*

○ *Faced with hurdles or mishaps, your instinct is to find solutions rather than lay blame. You shoulder the accountability for the team's collective results, be it triumphs or trials, and readily share accolades with your team members.*

○ *When addressing underperformance, your approach is immediate and constructive, delving deep with questions to unearth and address underlying issues. You do not postpone these types of discussions.*

○ *Your leadership style is unwavering, be it in a physical office or a remote setting. You value genuineness, ensuring your interactions are characterized by real emotions and empathy.*

You're candid about any personal challenges you might be grappling with, acknowledging any constraints you may be facing. However, you actively explore how these challenges might be channelled positively in the workplace or, at the very least, how you can meet your role's demands. Prioritizing well-being and the interests of the organization and its stakeholders, you are forthright if ever you find yourself unable to meet those demands.

Your Private Workshop: Your Personalized Whole Human Leadership Style

---

**Take out your notebook.
Once again, read the prompts below and begin.**

Create your leadership moniker.

What are some keywords that describe how you would like to be known for the work you do? What would you like your stakeholders to be saying about you?

What are your core values? If you are still exploring this, use this as a chance to write down those that are on your mind.

What would you look like showing up as a Whole Leader?

---◇---

Create Your Personalized Whole Human Leader Statement

---◇---

Use your answers to the prompts above and all that you have absorbed in reading this book to create your personal statement.

Here is the outline, in a MadLibs style, to help you along:

"I, *[Your Name]*, am a *[Moniker]*, committed to *[Action Verb]* *[Noun]* by *[Emotionally Driven Adjective]* *[Value]* in *[Working Environment]*. My purpose is to *[Action Verb]* *[Positive Outcome]* for *[Stakeholder/Team/Company]* by *[Value-Driven Action]*. As a Whole Human Leader, I strive to *[Desired Behaviour]*, *[Desired Behaviour]*, and *[Desired Behaviour]* to create a *[Adjective]* and *[Adjective]* workplace, where *[Positive Outcome]* is our common goal."

Now, let's fill in the blanks:

◇ *[Your Name]: Your name.*

◇ *[Moniker]: The leadership moniker you created during the workshop.*

◇ *[Action Verb]: An action you are committed to taking.*

◇ *[Noun]: What you are taking action on.*

◇ *[Emotionally Driven Adjective]: An adjective that reflects the emotional aspect of your commitment.*

○ *[Value]: One of your core values that guides your leadership.*

○ *[Working Environment]: The context or setting in which you lead (e.g., your organization or team).*

○ *[Positive Outcome]: A desirable result of your leadership.*

○ *[Stakeholder/Team/Company]: Whom you are leading or serving.*

○ *[Value-Driven Action]: An action aligned with your core values.*

○ *[Desired Behaviour]: Three behaviours you aim to exhibit as a leader.*

○ *[Adjective]: Two adjectives describing the workplace you want to create.*

○ *[Positive Outcome]: Reiterate the desirable result from above.*

By way of example, here's my Whole Human Leadership statement using this formula:

"I, *Victoria Pelletier*, am *the Turtle*, committed to *inspiring positive change* by *passionately championing strong workplace leadership and culture, combined with diversity, equity, and inclusion, throughout my work as an executive, author, and keynote speaker*. My purpose is to *drive growth and excellence* for *my team and teams across the globe* by *using my voice to promote a culture of inclusivity and collaboration*. As a leader, I strive to *listen actively, empathize deeply*, and *communicate openly* to create a *supportive* and *vibrant* workplace where *innovation and collaboration* are our common goal."

How to Use Your Whole Human Leadership Statement

Creating your personalized Whole Human Leadership statement is a great way to help hold yourself accountable and build connections with your stakeholders. You may even help your team and colleagues create their own statements. We will get to that in the last chapter of the book.

1. Accountability

Your leadership statement is your North Star, a reminder of your commitment to yourself and those you lead. Use it as a regular touchstone to hold yourself accountable.

- **Morning reflection:** *Start your day by revisiting your leadership statement. Reflect on how your planned actions align with your commitments. Ask yourself, "How can I exemplify my statement today?"*

- **Goal-setting:** *When setting leadership goals, confirm they resonate with your statement. This ensures that your objectives remain true to your values and aspirations.*

- **Feedback and self-reflection:** *During performance evaluations, refer to your leadership statement to assess your progress. Seek feedback from your team on how well you are living up to it.*

2. Connection

Your Whole Human Leadership statement is a powerful tool for building connections with your team and stakeholders.

Here's how:

- **Share your statement:** *Openly share your statement with your team and stakeholders. This fosters transparency and helps others understand your vision and values.*

- **Team-building:** *Motivate your team to craft their own statements. This both empowers them and harmonizes their goals with your leadership approach.*

- **Lead by example:** *Demonstrate the behaviours mentioned in your statement daily. Your actions speak louder than words and can inspire your team to do the same.*

- **Communicate with transparency:** *Use your statement as a foundation for honest and open communication. When faced with challenges or dilemmas, refer to your commitment to guide decision-making.*

Your Whole Human Leadership statement serves as a potent instrument for accountability and connection in leadership. Embrace it, embody it, and champion authentic leadership. Your stakeholders will value your dedication to fostering a positive and mission-oriented work environment. As you evolve toward being Whole, your team's potential to excel will grow. The ethos you establish will ripple beyond your organization, sparking a movement that manifests as your followers transform into self-directed leaders themselves.

Chapter 8 Key Takeaways

○ *Developing the Turtle Anatomy will naturally enhance and complete your Executive Presence.*

○ *A team that is inclusive and rich in diversity helps give leadership styles of the past a modern upgrade.*

○ *Every Whole Human Leader has their own personalized approach. Be an original and celebrate the uniqueness of your Whole Human Leader statement.*

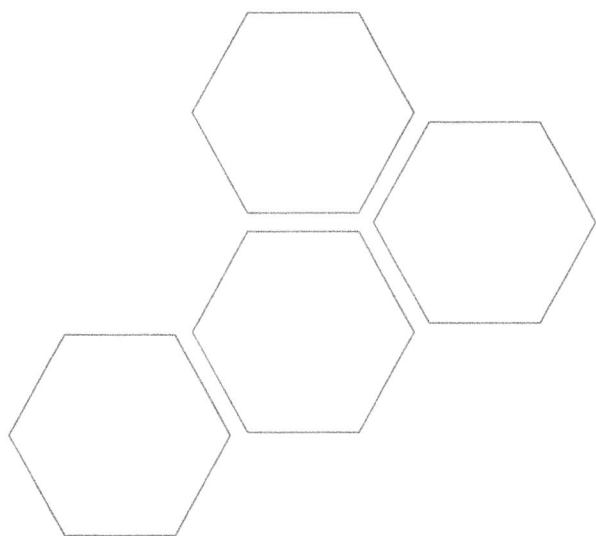

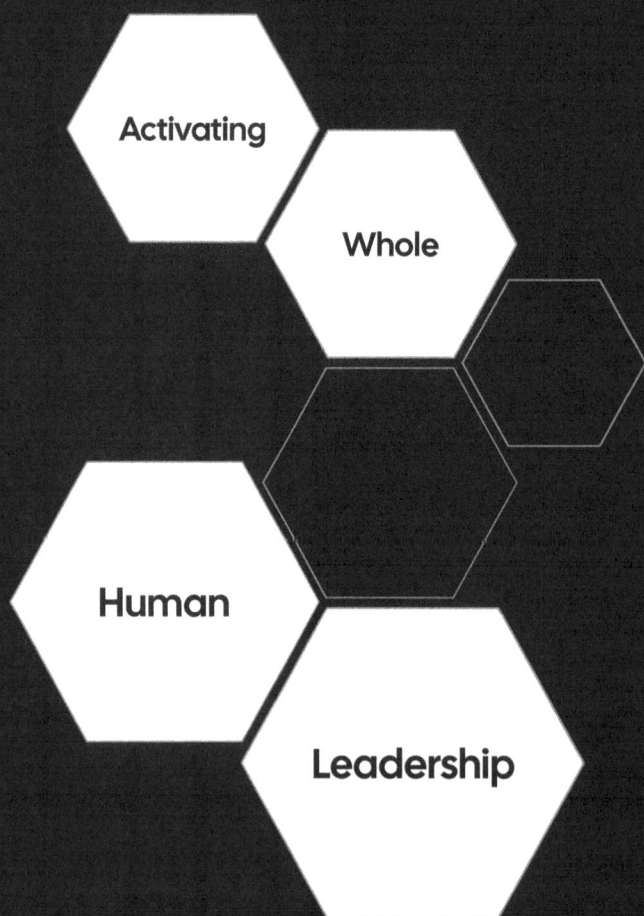

Activating

Whole

Human

Leadership

"People who are truly strong lift others up.
People who are truly powerful bring others together."

— Michelle Obama

Part **5**

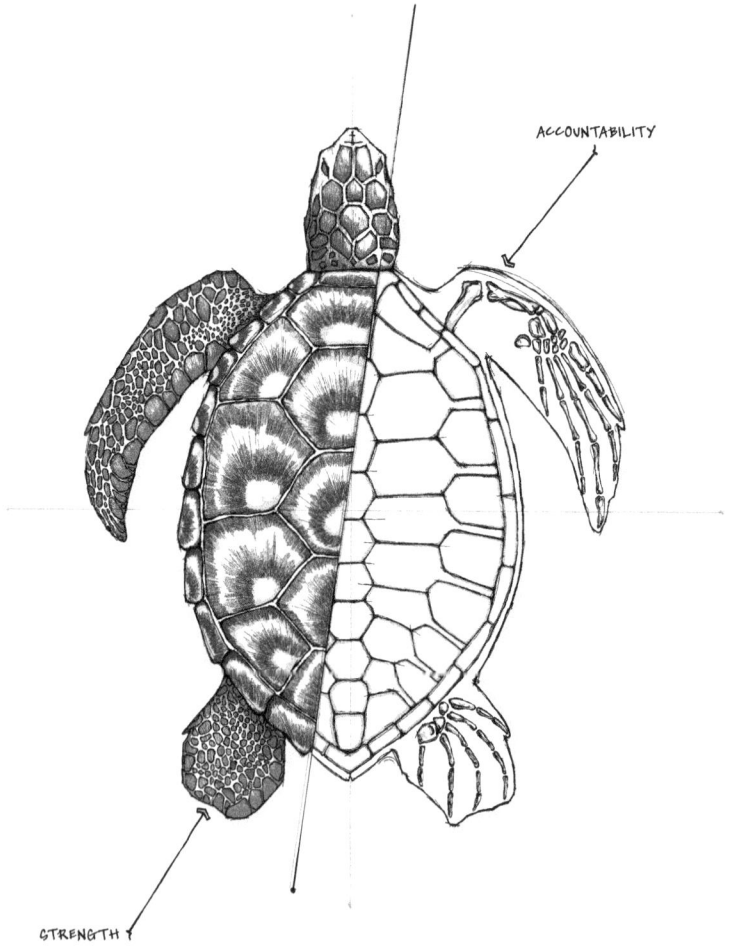

ACCOUNTABILITY

STRENGTH

Chapter 9

*High-Performing Teams and
Sustainable Leadership*

I 've never worked for a Turtle. I mention this fact because I want to reinforce how big the opportunity is for you right now to be a pioneer of Whole Human Leadership. Think of yourself as a successful product that is first to market, establishing the foundation for a new idea or a new industry by offering people an innovative solution that generates a massive amount of attention. Over time, you will evolve and eventually be replaced by another generation designed to provide even more features and an even better customer experience.

You won't be in this position forever. So, embrace this moment in time when employees are calling for a new style of leadership.

Whole Human Leadership is the solution to solving the very real and present pain point of employee lack of engagement and burnout, which has caused a workforce backlash that continues to negatively impact team performance.

Despite suffering the consequences of this workplace catastrophe, companies still aren't adapting at the pace and scale required to truly transform how leadership and teamwork are defined and complement each other. The business world needs bold, innovative leaders to step forward to force this change.

Who's responsible for *your* company's culture? You are.

While leadership teams are still scratching their heads, employees have already started changing your role as a leader for you. This is great news, by the way, because the people have spoken, and it is very clear what they want.

Given the organizational shift to more employee-centric models, focused on the wellness and engagement of employees, and considering the shortage of labour in key areas, employees have more leverage than ever before. Many of the 50 million workers who quit their jobs in 2022 are now getting rehired elsewhere, even with the current slowdown in the economy. They simply won't go back to more of the same as they search for job opportunities that offer purpose, impact, and a high degree of engagement with leadership.

Who is really leading right now? In many companies, employees are the ones driving change, not their leaders. But they cannot entirely manage the job of transformation by themselves because they lack something that you have. Authority.

Leaders are expected to produce outcomes primarily related to traditional business performance metrics like sales, revenue, and gross profit. Yet these do not necessarily coordinate with the outcomes expected by the team, which include improved work-life integration and flexibility, professional development opportunities, and a strong company culture. The only way to achieve the outcomes both stakeholder groups seek is through Whole Human Leadership.

Engagement is a term that is referenced often. At its core, the level of employee engagement is indicative of the emotional commitment and enthusiasm employees have toward their work, team, and organization. It's more than mere job satisfaction; it's an elevated state of diligence where employees are motivated to go above and beyond their basic job requirements. Engaged employees are invested in the company's goals, feel aligned with its values, and are likely to be more productive and loyal, and offer better customer service. Engagement is measured primarily through employee surveys. Given that you are in a leadership position, you have likely seen the survey results.

What about you? What do the results say?

How engaged are *you* with your team?

The bar you set for your own engagement should outpace what you'd expect from your team. Essentially, lead by example and aim for a level that's higher than what you'd ask your employees to reach.

My previous Iron Maiden persona certainly drove positive results, at least in terms of traditional business measurements. However, my team engagement score was severely lacking. I simply wasn't connecting with my team to understand their individual goals and motivations. I was driving them, yes, but toward what? Burnout? I did not spend time meeting with them to assess anything more than metrics and the fulfillment of their role. Back then, I was working in business process outsourcing, an industry where the majority of workers perform in a contact centre environment known for extremely high turnover. I lowered turnover and increased engagement, thus significantly improving the performance and financial results of the company (a big part of how I became known as the Turnaround Queen). But how much more could I have accomplished if I had been as fully engaged as the Turtle is? My old Iron Maiden self was simply unaware of this possibility.

---○---

Become the Accountable Leader

---○---

I considered filling this chapter with data points to support Whole Human Leadership, but I decided that if the state of the workforce today is not convincing enough for you, you are likely not ready for Whole Human Leadership. Still, I challenge you to move in the direction of the Turtle and experience how it feels when you fully engage.

Has leadership lost its lustre? In my view, it never had it to begin with. All of the imagery and ideals of leadership are based on a false narrative. Thinking about today's sorry state of leadership often makes me think of a speech given by Jimmy Carter back in 1979. In response to the severe energy crisis at that time, the speech turned out to be the President of the United States reading a litany of criticisms regarding his leadership. He had solicited this feedback in an all-out effort he made to get to the heart of what was happening in the country at that time. Examples include:

"Mr. President, you are not leading this nation. You are just managing the government."

"You don't see the people enough any more. Some of your cabinet members don't seem loyal."

"There's not enough discipline among your disciples. Mr. President, we are in trouble. Talk to us about blood, sweat, and tears. If you lead, Mr. President, we will follow."

He read this feedback out loud on national television. He concluded that the country was in far more than an energy crisis. The country, he stated, was in a crisis of confidence.

His admission of his failures is an astounding example of the type of courage it takes to step up as a Whole Human Leader by taking full responsibility. Jimmy Carter was not a celebrated politician. Beyond the Oval Office, however, he persisted in becoming a global humanitarian and peacebuilder. Failure did not stop him. It defined him for the better in the Long Game of Leadership.

Are we in a new type of confidence crisis?

How confident are you that you can fulfill your role at the level required of a Whole Human Leader?

How can your failures inform your own personalized Whole Human Leadership style?

Engagement as a leader is your accountability, not the company's. This is the responsibility of a leader. If you are not getting up every day thinking about who you need to interact with and what barriers you need to remove to achieve success, you are likely your own version of the Iron Maiden.

If you don't see leadership as people first, it's time you do.

Increased leadership engagement is the *key* to team performance. Some leaders choose to focus on one single trait, like trust, as a way to drive performance. But when it comes to creating high-performing teams, I believe that everything is connected. By taking even the smallest steps to develop higher levels of EI and CT skills, you will naturally begin to recognize empathy and authenticity in yourself and others. That awareness will lead to your actively working to practice the behaviours of the Turtle, helping you navigate change, failure, and success through a long-term lens. Whole Human Leaders play the Long Game of Leadership, as discussed in Chapter 10, ultimately leading to being able to sustain positive business outcomes over time. The level at which you activate Whole Human Leadership will be equal to the level of connection that your team has with you, each other, the company, and your clients.

In Chapter 8, we emphasized that the journey begins with you. But diving deep into the anatomy of the Turtle isn't just a solo endeavour; it sets the stage for your collaborative work with your team. As you embrace your role as a Whole Human Leader, you'll intuitively discern both the gaps and strengths within your team. This insight paves the way for reigniting trust and leveraging their collective prowess. By leading authentically, you'll not only inspire but also empower your team to forge ahead with boldness.

Your team doesn't want to quit quietly; they simply lack the clout you possess to instigate change. This undercurrent of revolt and backlash stems from that. Show them that their efforts to push for change are acknowledged and appreciated. By investing in them both personally and professionally, you're signalling they don't have to force the issue any longer. Demonstrate to them that you're now an ally in the effort.

Unlike the 50 million workers who quit their jobs in 2022 to make a statement for their personal health and happiness, you aren't allowed to quit. That's the difference in being a leader. I don't mean that you aren't allowed to quit your company. I mean that you are not allowed to stop moving. Not if you want to be the Turtle. You must always be looking to improve employee engagement and organizational culture. If you are not leading a team, you must lead yourself to new opportunities to drive the cultural change that we need in the workforce today.

Because you are in a position of power *and* authority, you have choices that you make every single day that are a testament to whether you are doing the right thing for the stakeholders. You also have a great deal of pressure to deliver results. How you go about it will determine if you can deliver positive outcomes for all stakeholders.

The Two Ways to Drive Business Outcomes

1. The Incomplete Leadership Approach

The world has tried and tested the Incomplete approach, and the Iron Maiden is being forced into retirement by worker backlash. In leaving the Iron Maiden behind, you'll notice a dramatic shift within yourself because you are now acting from an internal guidance system based on authenticity. You will be pleasantly surprised by how much easier the hard work feels when operating this way.

If you are like me, hard-wired to hustle, evolving from the Iron Maiden to the Turtle does not mean that you graduate from hard work. In fact, the world needs people like you and me who are passionate about our work and committed to getting results. The difference is simply that of being extreme versus being intentional. Put in the effort, yes, but not to the detriment of you and your team's long-term performance and satisfaction.

The Iron Maiden's way of driving results is all about spurts of intense, short-term gain producing long-term dissatisfaction that ultimately drives burnout. It is turn and burn, and all of us are just cogs that can be easily replaced. It's a reactive and chaotic leadership style that is self-sabotaging in the long run because it damages your reputation over time. With the Incomplete approach, success is defined *only* by numbers. You can achieve bottom-line results, but it will not be sustainable, especially in 2024 and beyond.

2. The Whole Human Leadership Method

The Whole Human Leadership method drives results using the unique framework of the Turtle. Along the journey, it brews trust and bolsters confidence, laying the foundation for lasting achievements and profound cultural shifts. By tapping into the purpose and passion of each team member, the Turtle method multiplies efficacy. The magic unfolds when everyone acknowledges that the team is the company's crown jewel, and leadership sets the gold standard in engagement. Leadership here doesn't just lead; they exemplify. And why does it last? Because it's holistic and thorough.

The exodus of workers in 2022, along with the silent but significant departures of key contributors, underscores a pressing need. Their clarion call? An urgent need for a new, more engaged type of leadership: Whole Human Leadership. Those Unseen Employees, who often match or even surpass the dedication of your top talent, are striving to emerge from the shadows, eager to ascend.

The supply of Whole Human Leaders is low.

We keep talking about a labour shortage, but in actuality, the issue is that we have a shortage of effective leaders who understand the need to change to attract and retain great talent. It's not that employees don't want to work anymore. They simply don't want to work for Incomplete Leaders.

Leaders who shield their vulnerabilities, overlook their team's viewpoints, or breeze past team members without truly acknowledging them simply aren't engaged. If you're not wholeheartedly invested in both the individual triumphs and collective victories of your team and company, then how can you anticipate glowing feedback on that survey?

You might be starting at version 1.0, but the advent of Whole Human Leadership is happening, and before we know it, with more leaders on board, it will only take a few years for version 5.0 to be released. There are always new layers to uncover as a Whole Human Leader. Isn't that exhilarating? You get to be a part of this massive, unprecedented transformation in the workforce by defining the features of the future now.

My hope is that once you finish this book, its impact lingers with you. You will see yourself as the moniker you aspire to become, and you will see everyone around you as essential to your success as a leader.

Have you ever poured your energy into persuading someone, only to be met with walls of defence? Yet, sometime later—be it weeks or years—they ring you up, expressing how your words sparked a positive shift in them? Or perhaps you've been on the receiving end, initially resisting but later finding truth in what was shared.

Such moments are intrinsic to our human journey and are especially pivotal as we evolve into the Whole Human Leaders we aim to be. Transformation might feel like a slow dance. My own metamorphosis from the Iron Maiden to the Turtle spanned more than a decade. And guess what? The journey of growth never truly ends.

While it took me that long, the lessons I share are intended to ensure that it takes you much less time to get there.

The workforce crisis has reached unprecedented levels. Whole Human Leadership should no longer be seen as a valiant, heroic move. It should be the default mode of leadership all leaders aspire to. But to get there, it must become a movement driven by your influence.

That is my goal in writing this book. The state of the workforce is dependent on leaders like you who are committed to creating change for themselves as the basis for cultural transformation.

The process can and will feel uncomfortable at points along the way, like back when I had to remind myself to stop and pause from my "all business all of the time" mode to take five minutes at the start of meetings to connect on a human level with my colleagues. As results begin to manifest, you'll find that your attention shifts away from the immediate and zeroes in on the lasting legacy you're creating.

As the Turtle, you might not always grasp the full scope of your influence. Whole Human Leadership is deeply rooted in serving and prioritizing the well-being of your team and the greater good of the company. When you immerse yourself in holistic leadership, taking responsibility and advocating for what's best for the team, the immediate outcomes might be evident. However, the ripple effect of your impact might require a longer horizon to fully reveal itself.

When Roger informed me that he had made partner, I was overjoyed to have been a part of his journey. He chose me as a leader with whom he could share his dreams, somebody with whom he could create waves of positive emotional contagion through the work that he did in reverse mentoring. Even though I left the company, my relationship with Roger has remained strong.

After the actions I took and the responsibility I assumed in my role working with Kate, I left her knowing that she could trust someone younger and less experienced than herself, and I took my experience with Kate as a win that taught me that patience and consistency do prevail.

Teams that are truly engaged witness fewer departures, boast increased productivity, enjoy richer profit margins, and earn rave reviews from customers. But this isn't just about the present moment. This is about shaping the future of work. It's your opportunity to redefine it, crafting a lasting legacy for the upcoming waves of leaders.

This book is a tapestry of personal tales about evolving into a Whole Human in the professional realm. My aim? To illuminate your path, demonstrating that you have the power to refine, reset, or radically transform your leadership approach, all in the name of enduring success.

Chapter 9 Key Takeaways

Embracing Whole Human Leadership is a game-changer for both leaders and their teams, paving the way for the success everyone's aiming for.

With the reins of power and authority in your hands, it's on you to make choices that benefit all your stakeholders. It's all about doing the right thing.

The true scarcity we're facing isn't in the workforce but ineffective leadership. Seize this chance to revamp your leadership style and stand out.

Don't expect overnight wonders when you start integrating Whole Human Leadership traits. Stick with it, and the rewards will unfold over time, making a meaningful difference.

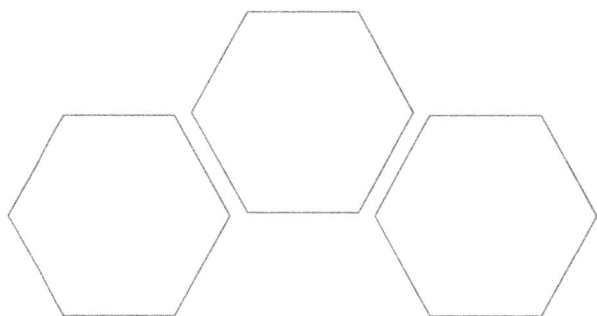

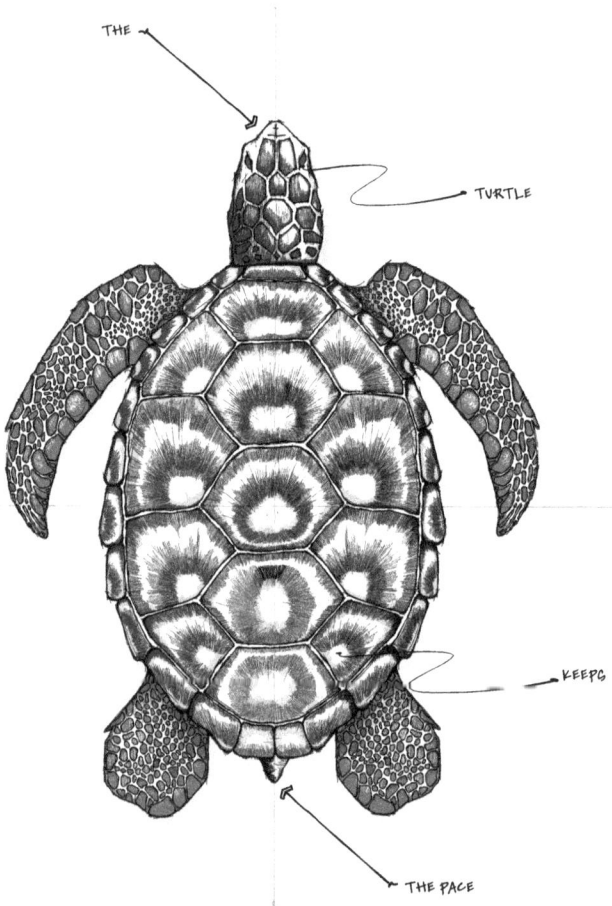

THE

TURTLE

KEEPS

THE PACE

*Keeping Pace: The Long
Game of Leadership*

Recently, I was contacted by an ex-colleague regarding mentoring one of her co-workers, a trans male, experiencing significant discrimination at work. Nick, named Nicole prior to transitioning, wanted mentorship on how to effectively advocate for himself and he also sought coaching for future career progression.

I met with Nick, and he shared with me that his employer did not allow him to use either the men's or the women's washrooms on his floor. Instead, he was forced to use the accessible washroom located on another floor. He also told me about his once being asked, in front of senior leaders and clients, "What are you?" On top of all of this, his employer refused to use his preferred name, Nick, and the pronouns he/him/his. I offered advice and language to help him craft a complaint to his human resources department and provided the names of several employment lawyers.

Nick was also struggling to translate his new gender identification into how he was showing up professionally. His resume, for example, still used the name Nicole, but his LinkedIn profile photo depicted his masculine identity. Nick and I discussed who he wanted to show up as at work and how he wanted to be known and seen. I worked with him on aligning his needs with his actions so he could present his authentic self to his peers and prospective employers.

Subsequently, Nick did discover and develop an authentic workplace expression of himself, which stimulated him to leave the company to forge a more positive path for himself, one where he doesn't worry about not feeling included or not having a strong sense of belonging with his colleagues.

As time has gone on and my work has unfolded, I have come to understand that the work of a Whole Human Leader is not confined to the context of a particular role inside a single company. I now relish being called on to provide advice and professional guidance for people like Nick, helping people whom I would not have met if I had not created a followership based on my core values.

The Long Game of Leadership

Whole Human Leadership paves the way for enduring cultural transformation. The practices and skills rooted in the Turtle Anatomy aren't just fleeting tactics; they're life-long commitments, permeating every facet of our existence. This approach not only fosters a tapestry of workplace diversity and inclusion but also champions well-being, leading to positive ripples across business results.

Whole Human Leadership isn't just about the present moment and need. It's also what you leave behind as you evolve. And it's about the legacy you create, fostering a future filled with thriving businesses and shared economic prosperity.

The Long Game of Leadership extends well beyond your tenure at any given company, with each day providing a small contribution to your ever-accumulating leadership legacy. While your workplace may evolve or change altogether, your commitment to the enduring journey of leadership should remain unyielding.

There are many ways you can play the Long Game of Leadership beyond your official corporate role: you can focus on educating, providing personal and professional development and mentoring, authoring blogs or even a book, or sharing your experience and ideas at workshops and conferences. When your purpose echoes consistently across every aspect of your life, it amplifies the impact you aspire to make on the world.

As a keynote speaker, I have had the great fortune of helping people in the audience that I would have otherwise not met. Through my various media appearances, I have been given a platform to talk about important issues in business and leadership that range from LGBTQ+ rights to speaking out about inequity for women and people of colour.

My media and speaking platforms have made my personal story accessible to the world, and have created connections with others that have allowed me to attract and inspire a followership. This network has made the changes I want to make in the world become far more expansive and possible.

The Long Game of Leadership is a natural by-product of the evolution of the Turtle. When you lead with a relentless commitment to your core values, the journey is boundless. You cannot imagine how many people are watching and being influenced by you. It's a never-ending journey, but with steadfastness and resilience, your odds of leaving a lasting imprint grow. Even if you touch just one life on this path, the commitment to doing right proves its worth.

―――――◇―――――

Transitions

―――――◇―――――

You will experience times of transition during your career. You may face tough choices when deciding whether it's time to part ways with an organization. No matter your choice, as a Whole Human Leader you'll uphold professional grace, drawing strength from the Turtle anatomy. The thoughtful, intentional manner in which you conclude your chapter with a company underscores the enduring spirit of the Long Game of Leadership.

As a Whole Human Leader, there are three main reasons you might decide to transition or complete your employment.

1. Misalignment of Core Values

When I confronted fraud with the CEO in the story I referenced in Chapter 3, I was confronted by a clear and dangerous contradiction of ethics that, without question, meant that I had to leave. That was an example of a situation where I could not and did not compromise my values. It was also a clear example of how a misalignment of core values means that your departure will likely be swift.

In situations like this, I have found that the best strategy is to make it very clear, both verbally and in writing, the reasons for your departure. The Turtle doesn't leave without sticking out its neck, communicating the misalignment of core values or wrongdoing before departing.

2. Recruitment to Another Organization

Great leaders receive many calls from recruiters looking to woo them to another organization. This type of transition can serve as a route to leading at a higher level, creating even more impact than before. A positive by-product of being vocal and publicly committed to your core values is that the right companies, those attuned to your beliefs and priorities, are more likely to seek you out because you have made it very clear what you stand for.

Oftentimes, I have been called by CEOs who say that they want to create a more diverse and inclusive culture but struggle to do so because their network is made up of people who often perpetuate pattern matching. Given my public platform, they expect me to be honest and recommend a new way forward. I am always willing to engage with them, even though the effort doesn't always produce a true willingness on their part to do something different (but often it does).

The Turtle can positively impact more organizations with the right strategy. When leaving one organization to make a difference in another, the one thing that I make sure of, aside from fulfilling my role through my final day of employment, is that I have left aspiring Turtles behind to increase the odds that the work I did will have a positive and lasting effect on the company.

3. You Have Fulfilled Your Role to the Fullest Extent

I had to be intentional and strategic when it came to deciding the timing of my resignation from the company led by the CEO with the mentality that I believed cutting a thousand team members was good practice. For the good of the team, I knew

I had to finish the work that I was doing to finalize the acquisition that had taken place. I refused to compromise my values, asserting that while I wouldn't support further cuts, I was committed to seeing the job through to its end.

In those negotiations, I believed I was acting in the best interest of both the company and its employees. Leaving prematurely would have felt like a failure on my part. Once the acquisition was complete, I recognized that my leadership style might not mesh well with the prevailing style in the long haul. It was time to move on.

During times of transition, when I've decided it's time to move on from a company, I make sure before I leave to do right by everyone involved to the best of my ability. Upon tendering my resignation, I pledge to meet certain objectives and collaborate with leadership for a smooth and professional transition. My main motivation in this is to help the *people* I am leaving behind, more so than the organization. I believe it's an integral part of Whole Human Leadership.

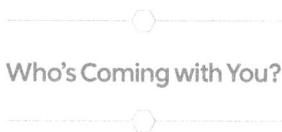

Who's Coming with You?

Your team is more than just your direct reports. It also includes those in the audience when you are on stage and those across the screen during a video call. It even includes the people waiting for you at the end of the day at home, like my husband, Dany, or my best friend Jen, both of whom see me whole at home, which is so vital in helping me present my whole self at work.

The Turtle embodies its essence, effortlessly presenting its whole, real self. You shine when you are the Turtle, embracing authenticity and shedding unnecessary burdens, making yourself more visible to those who matter most in every corner of your life. When you no longer conceal your true self in professional settings, your leadership transforms into a powerful force that permeates your entire existence. Both your team and your loved ones become the circle of influence that you always aspired to have. It's the people you draw in who eventually shape the lasting mark you aim to leave on the world.

I *know* Whole Human Leadership works. I have twenty years of receipts to prove it: recording the video for Roger in support of his promotion to partner after I left the company, receiving the call from Mary asking for me to serve as an employment reference and the thousands of people who have reached out to me seeking support.

The testament to your leadership capabilities is reflected in the individuals who gravitate toward you. Whether it's potential Turtles I encounter during my speaking events or Turtle leaders I meet within my professional networks, the demand is evident. The global stage yearns for leaders who resonate with both the whispered and pronounced needs of the workforce. Aligning with fellow leaders passionate about fostering immense value through enduring cultural shifts is pivotal for genuine and lasting movement. Given your position at the table, you're primed to sculpt a legacy in Whole Human Leadership.

Become a member of a network of leaders who are aligned with your core values, and schedule those one-on-one meetings with indirect reports that you may not yet have met, and with those you haven't seen in some time. Make a list of the places you can discover the *who* and step into the arena.

As long as you hold the seat, you hold the responsibility.

Small Acts of Whole Human Leadership

A few months back, I received a business book authored by a respected professional friend titled *Wrong Fit, Right Fit: Why How We Work Matters More Than Ever*.[20] The thought crossed my mind one day that some of the leaders in one of my networking groups who were struggling through their own career transitions might appreciate it if I gifted them the book. In addition, it would help me support my friend, the author, Dr. André Martin.

After reaching out through the member platform, I sent some of the women in the group the book. A few weeks later, I received a card in the mail. It read: "I appreciate your continued generosity to me and other women in all you do. I admire that you don't just talk the talk. You walk the walk. I feel so fortunate to be getting to know you. Thanks again." I didn't gift the book to receive anything in return; however, this note validated why I remain so committed to this way of being.

After realizing that I had missed National Coming Out Day because I was having a rough week, I posted this message in the LGBTQ+ group chat I formed in my networking group: "I just realized it was National Coming Out Day yesterday. I normally post publicly on the day, but I've been feeling a bit deflated, so I'll cheer on everyone else's posts. Hugs to all."

"You do such a great job of supporting everyone else. Is there anything we can do for you today?" replied one of the members. Her response warmed my heart.

This is the type of collective support that shows up in Whole Human Leadership. You will no longer feel alone or isolated, and you will no longer fear showing emotion, admitting failure, or openly sharing your lived experiences with others.

In my experience, strengthening what exists has been a

rewarding part of Whole Human Leadership. As an example, I proudly accepted a position with a company that had done some great work to create a diverse team. In fact, I had the most diverse team across the company globally. While a lot of the employees were already in their roles when I arrived, I was able to shift the dialogue and shift their engagement. Having one of the teams with the highest engagement results, as administered in the annual employee engagement survey, was a huge win for all.

Time and time again, in the positions that I have held in my career, internal employee surveys have come back indicating that my teams have been generally happier than others within the organization. These results are truly meaningful to me. Yes, it is business metrics such as sales, revenue, and profitability that I am measured on and that my annual performance bonus is mainly weighted toward. Yet I feel that what drives my performance in those traditional metrics is my Whole Human focus on leading my team to their best possible effort. That is the true results multiplier and the real reason behind my success.

The incredible followership that I now have is, in part, composed of people who I have helped become leaders themselves. That's the legacy I want for myself—but more than that, I want it for you too.

That's the stuff that brings me joy.

I do what I do. And I do it with voracity because that's success for me.

What does success as a Whole Human Leader look like for you?

Through each small action, you demonstrate the meaning of your personalized Whole Human Leadership statement. But beyond that, commit yourself to going to great lengths to make Whole Human Leadership the new normal going forward. The only reason to look back is to learn.

Take the positive and negative feedback you have received and come forth with responsibility like Jimmy Carter did and cement the trust of your stakeholders.

Do you know the difference between effect and impact?

Impact happens on a larger scale.

Keep the pace and remember that the quiet quitters are looking for leaders who are no longer trying to prove something. They are trying to move something.

Chapter 10 Key Takeaways

Mastering the Turtle anatomy's skills and behaviours isn't just good practice—it's what the future of leadership demands.

When you let your authentic self shine in the professional world, your leadership becomes a beacon, inspiring others and enriching every aspect of your life.

The thoughtful way in which you conclude your time with a company underscores the enduring spirit of the Long Game of Leadership.

Staying aligned with your core values is a decision you'll never second-guess.

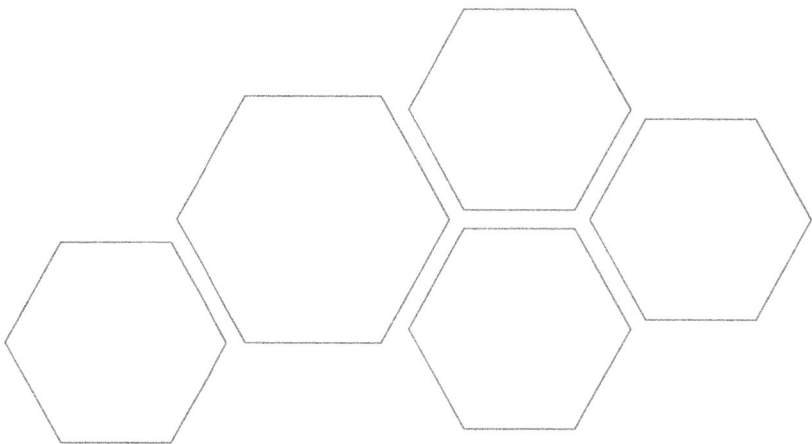

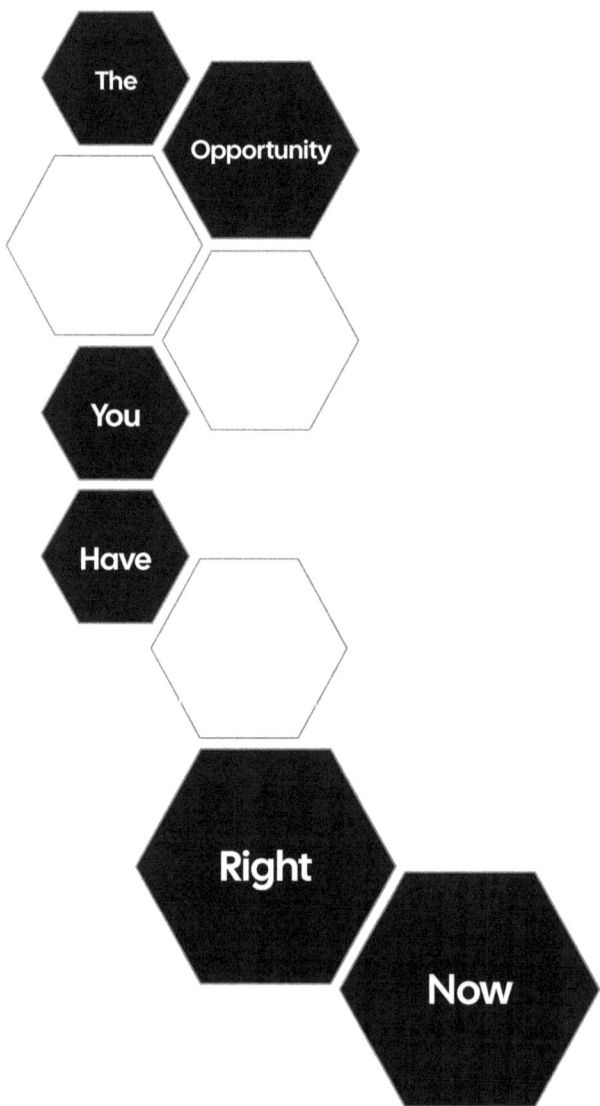

The Opportunity You Have Right Now

Conclusion

*The Opportunity You
Have Right Now*

As we reach the culmination of this journey into the realm of Whole Human Leadership, it's imperative to grasp the profound impact of our choices. Every day, we are confronted with a myriad of behavioural choices, each representing an opportunity to steer leadership in the right direction.

Whole Human Leadership is not merely a concept or a theory; it is a call to action. It beckons us to rise above the mundane, break free from the confines of old paradigms, and to embrace a future where leadership is synonymous with authenticity, empathy, and unwavering commitment to doing what is right.

We stand at the crossroads of transformation, and the responsibility falls on the shoulders of Whole Human Leaders like you to forge our collective path forward. You possess the power to infuse organizations with purpose, to inspire teams with compassion, and to ignite the flames of change with your unwavering dedication.

In the labyrinth of life, remember that you are not alone. The Turtle, with its resilient spirit, steadfastly moves forward, setting the pace and guiding us all toward a future where leadership is a force for good. Whole Human Leadership transcends boundaries, and it starts with you.

So, as you close the final chapter of this book, don't let it be the end of your journey but the beginning of your legacy. It's time to seize the opportunity before you, armed with the wisdom of Whole Human Leadership and the unwavering determination to make a difference.

The world eagerly awaits the impact of people like you, who lead from the heart, who understand the intricate dance between critical thinking and emotional intelligence, and who are committed to the journey of becoming better leaders, and better humans.

Now is your moment. Embrace it with the spirit of the Turtle, and let your leadership shine as a beacon of hope, inspiration, and transformation. Together, we will create a world where Whole Human Leadership is the new norm—a world that we can all be proud to pass on to future generations.

Thank you for embarking on this transformative journey.

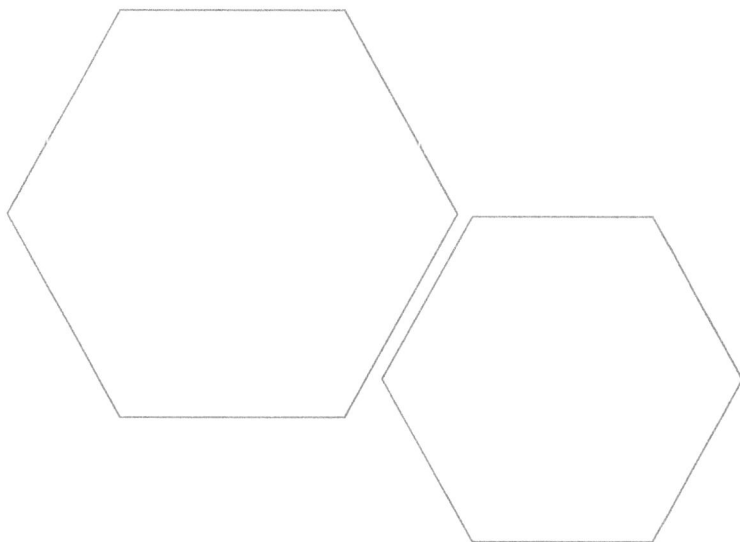

The future of leadership is in your hands.

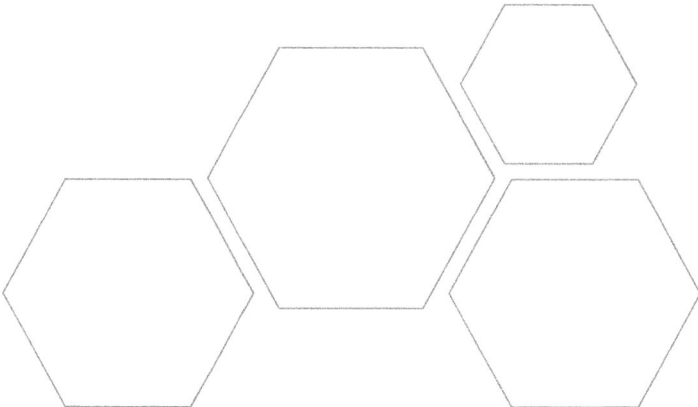

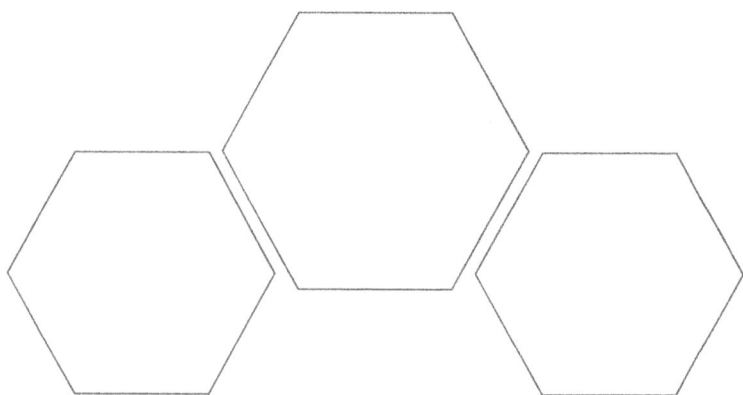

Recommended Reading

I am an avid reader, with my preferred method of learning being audiobooks and podcasts these days. There are so many titles that I considered recommending here, but I decided to share with you a few that have been most consequential and meaningful to me.

The Power of Vulnerability: Teachings on Authenticity, Connection, and Courage, by Brené Brown. In this book, Brown delves deep into the power of vulnerability and how it can transform the way we live, love, parent, and lead.

Dare to Lead: Brave Work. Tough Conversations. Whole Hearts, by Brené Brown. This book emphasizes the importance of vulnerability in leadership, encouraging leaders to embrace their imperfections and lead with empathy and courage.

Start with Why: How Great Leaders Inspire Everyone to Take Action, by Simon Sinek. *Start with Why* emphasizes the importance of understanding the "why" behind what we do, which is key to inspirational leadership.

The Infinite Game, by Simon Sinek. Sinek presents the idea of business and leadership as an ongoing journey, emphasizing the importance of continuous improvement over the pursuit of finite goals. He advocates for an "infinite mindset," which equips leaders to navigate change and uncertainty, fostering resilience and long-term success.

Hidden Potential: The Science of Achieving Greater Things, by Adam Grant. Grant's book offers a new framework for raising aspirations and exceeding expectations, highlighting the importance of designing systems that create opportunities for those people often underrated and overlooked.

Wrong Fit, Right Fit: Why How We Work Matters More Than Ever, by Dr. André Martin. In this book, Dr. Martin discusses the importance of finding the right fit in both personal and professional contexts. The book provides insights into how misalignment can be detrimental and how finding the right fit can lead to greater success and fulfillment.

Radical Candor: Be a Kick-Ass Boss Without Losing Your Humanity, by Kim Scott. Focused on the concept of radical candor, this book provides practical advice on how to balance directness with empathy in leadership.

Mindset: The New Psychology of Success, by Carol S. Dweck. Dweck's research on fixed and growth mindsets is crucial for leaders who want to foster an environment of continuous learning and resilience.

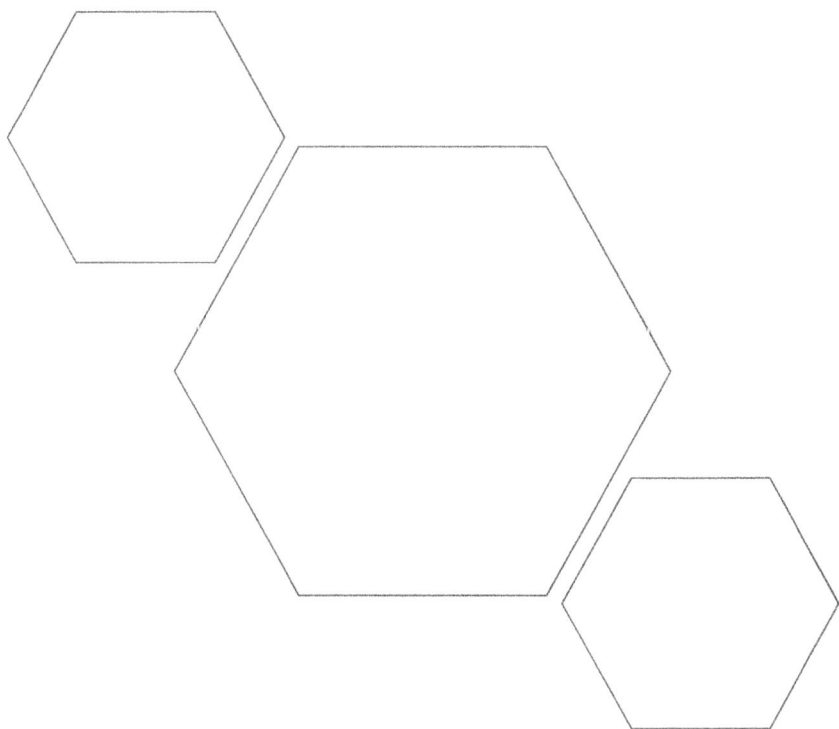

Notes

1. Iacursi, G. "2022 was the 'real year of the Great Resignation,' says economist." February 2023. CNBC. https://ww.cnbc.com/2023/02/01/why-2022-was-the-real-year-of-the-great-resignation.html (2)

2. Davis, D. "Women-founded startups raised 1.9% of all VC funds in 2022, a drop from 2021." January, 2023. Tech Crunch + Market Analysis. https://tcrn.ch/3ZPhfHl.(4)

3. Tennant, E. "How the philosophy behind the Japanese art form of kintsugi can help us navigate failure." November 2022. The Conversation. https://theconversation.com/how-the-philosophy-behind-the-japanese-art-form-of-kintsugi-can-help-us-navigate-failure-193487 (5)

4. Mahand, T., Caldwell, C. "Quiet Quitting—Causes and Opportunities." 2023. *Business and Management Research.* https://www.sciedupress.com/journal/index.php/bmr/article/view/23116. (5)

5. Bogen, M. "All the Ways Hiring Algorithms Can Introduce Bias." May 2019. *Harvard Business Review.* https://hbr.

org/2019/05/all-the-ways-hiring-algorithms-can-introduce-bias. (43)

6. Hewlett, S., Marshall, M., Sherbin, L., *How Diversity Can Drive Innovation.* December 2013. Harvard Business Review. (43)

7. WILL McPHAIL. (n.d.). WILL McPHAIL. https://www.will-mcphail.com/store/tyb4jgvohv7i1c37ksnclmsba6a368 (44)

8. Fuller, J., Raman, M., Sage-Gavin, E., Hines, K., et al. *Hidden Workers: Untapped Talent.* September, 2021. Harvard Business School Project on Managing the Future of (45)

9. Dwyer, C.P. *Critical Thinking: Conceptual Perspectives and Practical Guidelines.* 2017. Cambridge University Press. (61)

10. Dwyer, C.P., Hogan, M.J., & Stewart, I. "The evaluation of argument mapping-infused critical thinking instruction as a method of enhancing reflective judgment performance." 2015. *Thinking Skills & Creativity.* (62)

11. Tomaszek, K. "Do positive emotions prompt people to be more authentic? The mediation effect of gratitude and empathy dimensions on the relationship between humility state and perceived false self." (2022). Current Issues in Personality Psychology. 11. 10.5114/cipp.2022.116363. (83)

12. Leading Effectively Staff. "The Importance of Empathy in the Workplace." January 2023. Center for Creative Leadership. https://www.ccl.org/articles/leading-effectively-articles/empathy-in-the-workplace-a-tool-for-effective-leadership/. (85)

13. McKinsey & Company. "Diversity Wins: How Inclusion Matters."

May 2020. https://www.mckinsey.com/~/media/mckinsey/featured%20insights/diversity%20and%20inclusion/diversity%20wins%20how%20inclusion%20matters/diversity-wins-how-inclusion-matters-vf.pdf (118)

14. American Sociological Association. "Research links diversity with increased sales revenue and profits, more customers." EurekAlert! March, 2009. https://www.eurekalert.org/news-releases/875837. (119)

15. Liswood, L. "3 Reasons Why Business Leaders Can't Afford to Ignore Diversity." August 2019. World Economic Forum. https://www.weforum.org/agenda/2019/08/3-reasons-why-business-leaders-cant-afford-to-ignore-diversity/. (121)

16. Phillips, K. "How Diversity Makes Us Smarter." October 2014. *Scientific American.* (121)

17. Hewlett, S. *Executive Presence: The Missing Link between Merit and Success.* 2014. Harper Business. (150)

18. Frangos, C. "Female Leadership: The New Approach in the Workplace." October 2021. *Forbes.* https://www.forbes.com/sites/cassandrafrangos/2021/10/28/female-leadership-the-new-approach-in-the-workplace/ (151)

19. Sullivan, D. *Who Not How.* 2020. Hay House. (156)

20. Martin, A. *Wrong Fit, Right Fit: Why How We Work Matters More Than Ever.* 2023. IT Revolution Press. (200)

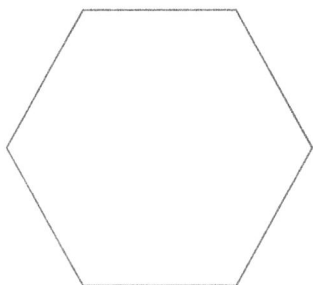

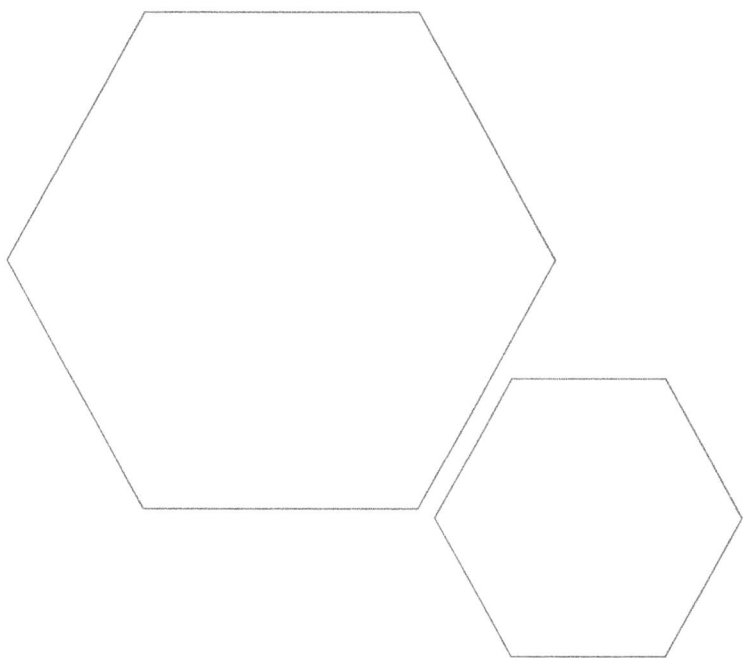

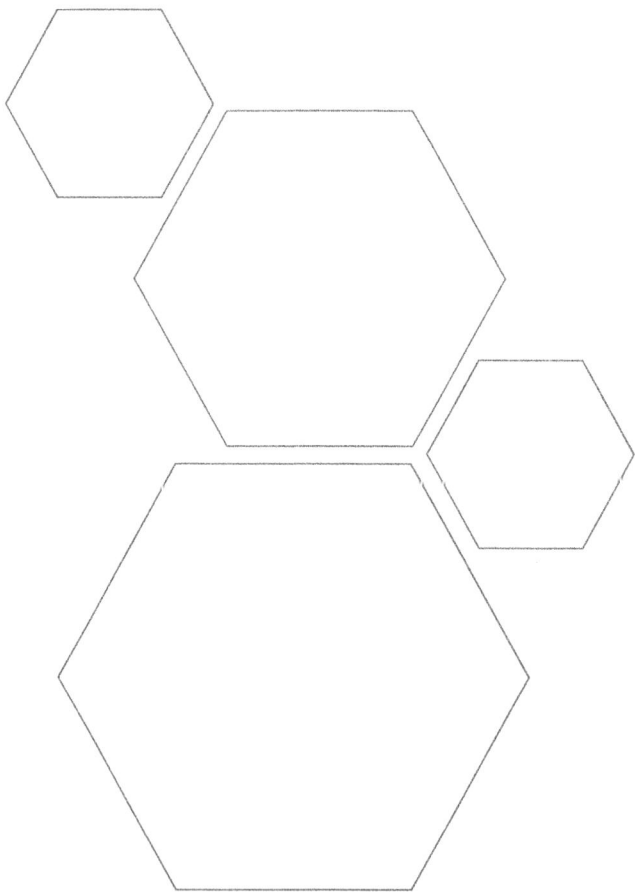

Acknowledgements

I n writing this book, I've come to appreciate the myriad of influences that have shaped my journey in leadership. Interestingly, I haven't had the privilege of many exemplary leadership role models, either in my personal life or in my career. I have learned much from a few, and I've had fantastic relationships with many others—but none taught me Whole Human Leadership. Nevertheless, working alongside numerous remarkable leaders has been enlightening, and I thank them for their positive influence on me. I also extend my gratitude to those who have exemplified less-than-ideal leadership (sometimes horrible, and a few quite unethical), because they have inadvertently contributed to defining my approach and philosophy.

A special note of appreciation goes to my now-deceased ex-wife, Dee. Her support during the nascent stages of my executive career was instrumental.

To Dany, my husband, who makes my endeavors in leadership, public speaking, and advocacy not only possible, but meaningful—you are my steadfast rock. You are an amazing partner who is not just good to me, but for me. As you said in our wedding vows, you are the "patience to my impatience." I love you fully.

My best friend, Jen, who knows me inside out and who gave me the very appropriate nickname, "Turtle," has always reminded me of the importance of being authentically myself. Your friendship allows me to embrace my true self, unfiltered and genuine. You are "my person."

Lastly, thanks go to my children, Zoë and Jordyn, who fill my life with boundless joy and purpose so strong that words can hardly capture it. You have enriched my journey in ways I could never have anticipated and continue to inspire me every day. I am so proud to be your mother.

Each of you, in your unique way, has left an indelible mark on my life and my work. Thank you for being part of my story.

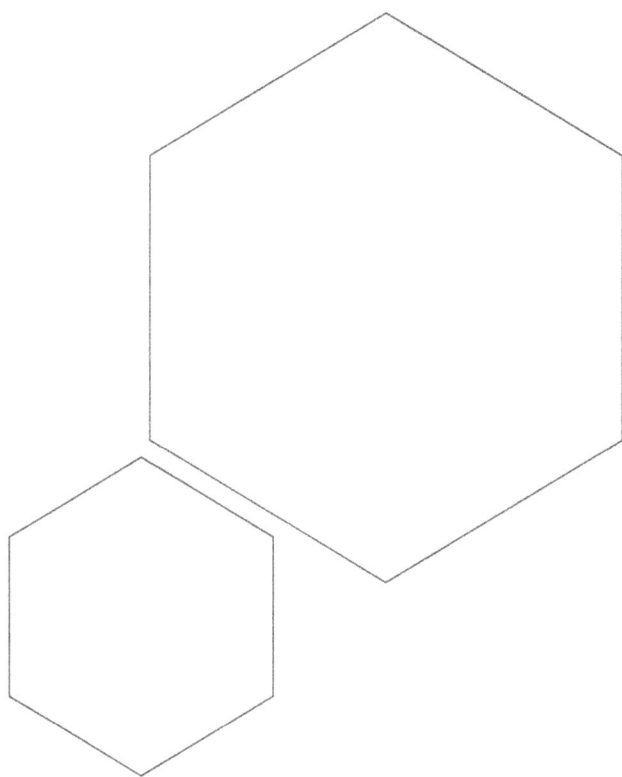

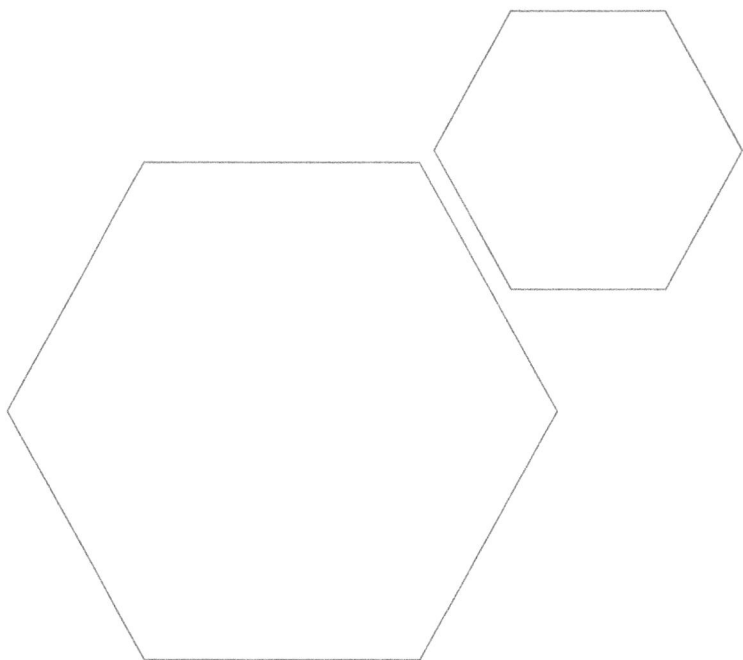

You may follow or connect
with Victoria via her website:

www.Victoria-Pelletier.com

About the Author

Victoria Pelletier is a seasoned corporate executive with over two decades of leadership experience, including roles as COO, President, and CEO. Her career has been marked by a passion for inspiring positive change and growth in organizations, a journey also defined by her commitment to continuous personal learning, growth, and resilience.

Victoria's contributions have earned her numerous awards and recognition for her dedication to and advocacy for diversity, equity, and inclusion, as well as for her significant history of mentorship in the workplace.

She is a sought-after media guest and professional keynote speaker. Victoria regularly shares her insights on topics such as Whole Human Leadership, developing resilience, and personal branding while always striving to inspire and empower others on their journeys.

Victoria's other books include *Unstoppable: Changemakers Who Dare to Make a Difference* and *Influence Unleashed: Forging a Lasting Legacy Through Personal Branding.*